SURPRISES AT THE TABLE

SURPRISES AT THE TABLE

Else Schardt

Surprises at the Table

For information, E-mail at surpatab@juno.com

Produced in the United States of America

Cover design: Mindy Schardt

ISBN:

Printed by BookMasters, Inc.
Mansfield, Ohio

For Ron

CONTENTS

ACKNOWLEDGEMENTS

Thanks to my colleagues, students, and neighbors in Papua New Guinea, who often gathered with us at mealtimes and taught us valuable, life-transforming lessons for our lives.

My deep gratitude goes to Professor Norma Cook Everist for her inspirational teaching and writings as well as her encouragement these past years. I am also grateful to my colleague Jim Brimeyer for reading this manuscript and encouraging me as an instructor. To my fellow-missionaries Dr. Dean and Dorothy Zweck, my heartfelt thanks for reading these stories and for being precious friends over vast distances and over many years.

I am also grateful to Tim Leonhart of BookMasters, Inc., for guiding me in preparing the manuscript for publication.

Special thanks to my daughter-in-law, Mindy Schardt, for designing the cover and for sharing her faith and love with our whole family.

To our children and their families—Joy and Jeff with Ross and Briana, Heidi and Joel with Beren and Saffie, Natalie and Pat with Kaitlynn and Payton, and Graham and Mindy with Avryn—thanks for continuing to provide wonderful times of community and surprises whenever we gather at their tables and ours.

Finally, special thanks go to my husband, Ron, for giving me unwavering love and support, for sharing surprises at the table with me for forty-four years, and for patiently helping me prepare the manuscript for publication.

Else Schardt

PREFACE

My family's history with the island of New Guinea began one hundred years ago, when my Australian grandparents traveled there in 1906 to serve as missionaries. My father was born in New Guinea in 1911, and twenty-nine years later, I was born there. Of our four children, two can claim Papua New Guinea as the land of their birth.

Through these generations, many events have changed the island and its people, including invasions and much destruction during World War Two, the spread of the Christian Gospel, a gold rush, earthquakes, volcanic eruptions, floods, and droughts. Nevertheless, despite rugged mountain ranges, lack of roads, and hundreds of languages, New Guinea's four million people worked valiantly and successfully toward achieving independence in September of 1975. At that time the country's name was changed to Papua New Guinea. The people—amazingly diverse in cultures, languages, crafts, and beliefs—taught my family many valuable lessons for our lives, lessons about food as well as family, life, death, the environment, and community.

We learned that as people shared their food and the inevitable conversation that went along with communal mealtimes, a corporate spirit among individuals was forged. The practice of eating together and talking together builds relationships. In the same way, God's table brings people together and forges community. My German colleague, Irmgard Horndasch, often said, "Tischgemeinschaft ist die letzte Gemeinschaft." (Table fellowship is the ultimate fellowship.)

This volume of stories provides the reader with a glimpse of unusual meal-time experiences, mainly in Papua New Guinea. At the same time, the reader catches glimpses into the country's wonderful people and timeless traditions.

I have kept the country's name as *New Guinea* in stories about events that took place before Independence, and have changed the name to *Papua New Guinea* for stories about events after Independence.

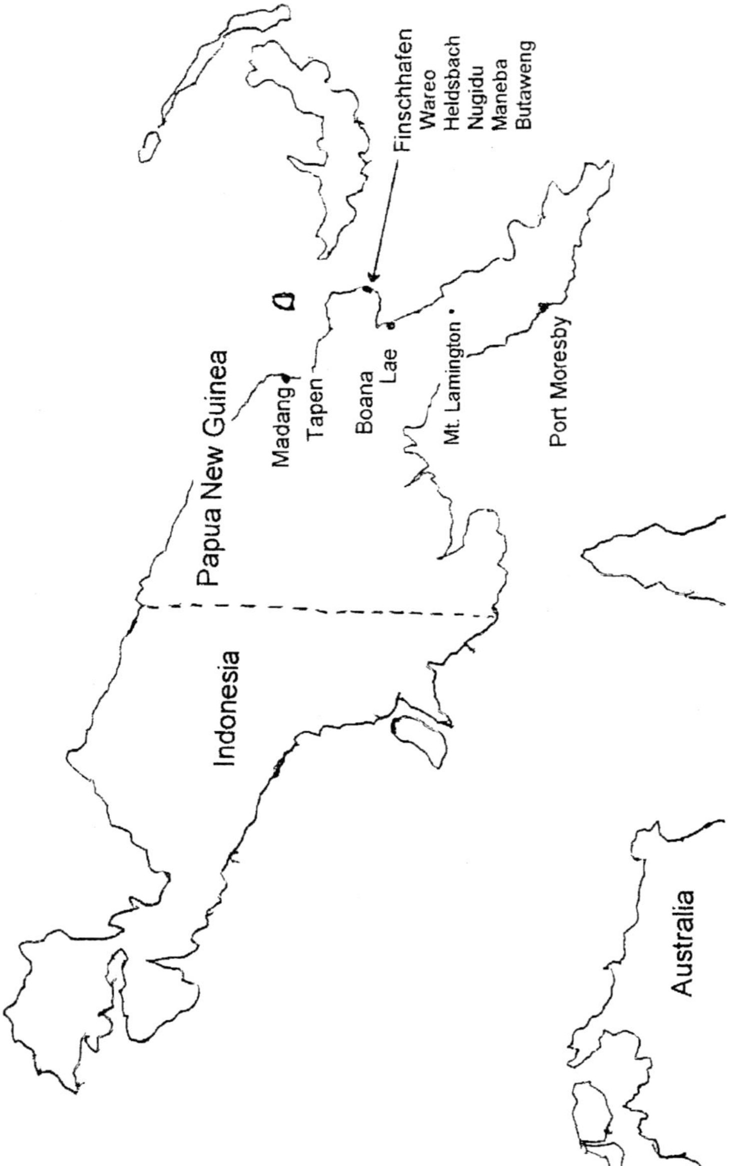

Map of New Guinea Island, and independent
country of Papua New Guinea

one

TABLES OF TRANSITION

New Guinea, the second largest island of the world, perches like a large bird above the northeastern tip of Australia's vast continent. A ruggedly mountainous, jungle-covered paradise located just south of the equator, New Guinea boasts a legendary assortment of trees, orchids, insects, and birds. Its hundreds of tribes of people speak more than eight hundred different languages and strive valiantly to work together for unity amid their incredible diversity of cultures.

Finschhafen, on New Guinea's Huon Peninsula, covers more than twenty miles of northeast coastline of the New Guinea Island. Diversity marks not only the people but also the shoreline. To the north nestle gorgeous white sand beaches interspersed with stretches of wild, jagged rocks where the surf crashes ceaselessly. Between these beaches appears a rare black sand beach, dangerously hot to bare feet and dotted with smooth round white stones looking like dumplings in a dark stew. Farther away from shore, shimmering green bays flanked by brilliant coral reefs give way to deep blue hues of the Pacific Ocean, endlessly fascinating visitors to this idyllic haven of the Pacific.

I was born in a spacious house at Kakoko, a medical outpost on a hill overlooking placid Finschhafen Harbor. My parents, Frieda and Martin Helbig, knew the place well, since Mother had worked at Kakoko before her marriage. Now they came back for the birth of their first child. Even though I don't remember the delivery table fashioned from hand-hewn local timbers, in later years I never tired of hearing the story of my birth: Mother's long journey to hospital on foot and by carriers down the jungle trails from Wareo; the doctor's order for her to go home again for a month since she was too early; Mother's onset of labor that very afternoon; the doctor's surprised looks; Sister Helene's assistance at the delivery; and my parents' excitement when they first saw me and heard me cry. Yes, there I lay on the first table of my life.

Unfortunately, this birthing table didn't last very long, for within a couple of years World War Two arrived on this gorgeous tropical island, and soon our hospital building was reduced to rubble, demolished by falling bombs.

My second table was a wooden table in my home in Wareo, where my parents worked as missionaries. Wareo sat in the mountains on a red clay nub of a jungle-covered range about three thousand feet above sea level. At this table my mother fed me my first solid food, and I promptly spat it all up. I kept growing, developing a pretty cheerful personality while juggling my two primary languages, German and Kotte. Here, many hours' travel from any road or store, Mother served simple nutritious meals for her little family. She brought in fresh vegetables from her garden, supplementing them with sweet potatoes, taro, yams, and other vegetables purchased from the village women. Many times she and I were the only persons at table, for Dad had to be on patrol much of the time, trekking and visiting villages and congregations dotted throughout the rugged area. At other times, visitors arrived on foot and on horseback, looking for food and respite. Mother regularly managed to find room and food for them.

Wareo remained my home for a heartbreakingly short time. In 1941, right after the bombing of Pearl Harbor during World War Two, the Australian government ordered expatriate women and children to leave New Guinea. Thus, Mother and I traveled to Australia while Dad had to remain on duty in Finschhafen. Soon after this, he was conscripted into the Australian army, and within a few months the Allies led a fierce battle in that area to recapture the peninsula Japanese troops had occupied earlier in the war. In one of the many ironic twists of war, the Allies, with whom Dad was serving and risking his life daily, bombed and destroyed our home in Wareo in order to flush out enemy troops. Thus, in one swift swoop of a bomber, our home, our shelter, our table, and many of our worldly possessions vanished. We became refugees. Fortunately, Dad had packed many of his precious theology and music books in plastic-lined boxes, and then he and some of his New Guinean coworkers had carried the boxes to the jungle. They'd buried some of the boxes underground while they had hidden others in a hut in the forest. In 1946, when my father was among the first group of missionaries allowed back into New Guinea, he hiked up the mountains to Wareo and recovered some of the boxes. Other crates were never found, however, since the men who buried them decided, for safety reasons, not to tell one another about the locations. Some of those brave men were killed in the war, carrying the secret with them.

As war refugees in Australia, we spent the first months living with my uncle and aunt in Queensland, and the immense table in their parsonage became the first table of my earliest memories. A lively, inquisitive toddler, I gained endless delight from watching my four older cousins, whose antics became my daily entertainment. Elise and August Simpfendorfer, our patient aunt and uncle, graciously shared their rooms, their food, and their lives with us while my mother helped out wherever possible, creating culinary delights for the double family and entertaining all of us children with her many songs and stories.

Finally, after what must have seemed like a very long period of time, Dad was repatriated from the army and sent to Australia as a civilian again. He helped out as a pastor in various parishes for the remainder of the war years, daily hoping to return to his beloved New Guinea at the very first opportunity.

Around my uncle and aunt's table in the parsonage I began to learn another language—English. My cousins communicated in a mixture of English and German, and our parents often spoke German with one another, for that was their mother tongue. With gradual exposure to congregation members and neighbors' children, I rapidly acquired the vocabulary essential for making new friends and talking nonstop much of the time.

Our time in Queensland in the parsonage held one of my happiest memories of early childhood—the birth of my sister, Doris, whom I adored. During our time in Queensland, Dad assisted as a pastor in that area, and after a couple of years we moved to South Australia, where we lived with my grandparents in a borrowed farm house for a number of months. By then the novelty of being refugees had really worn off, and my folks became very anxious to return to New Guinea and resume their missionary work that had been so cruelly interrupted by war. True, they would never own their own home, but a mission house in the rain forests of New Guinea sounded more like a home than a borrowed bedroom in someone else's house in Australia.

South Australia provided my earliest formal education, for during our days there I turned five and a few months later I began attending Light Pass Lutheran Day School near our temporary living quarters. That year also saw the arrival of our baby brother, Theo, and we "big" sisters doted on him every spare moment.

Impermanence continued to characterize our lives, as we packed suitcases again a few months later and began the long journey back to New Guinea. Dad had gone ahead some months earlier to assess the damage of war's destruction and to build some kind of a shelter which could become our home. By this time, Mother had developed diabetes and required insulin injections daily. This necessitated a request for the luxury of refrigeration to keep the insulin from going bad in a tropical locale.

Where would we find a family table now? Who would be around the table with us there? Our journey stalled for many weeks in Sydney, where several families camped in the home of our marvelously patient friends, Elsie and Arthur Kohn. They opened their hearts and homes for this motley bunch of homeless women and children, and once again a temporary table served as a vital gathering place for us. The bonds created with the Kohn family and our fellow-travelers during that seemingly interminable delay in Sydney have already spanned sixty years. We crowded around that solid table at mealtimes, finding something to eat every time, and finding our gentle, smiling host and hostess willing to be amicable with us yet one more day. We took turns in their only bathroom, and whenever the four walls became too small for such a crowd, Mother would take us for a long walk on the clean streets of Sydney. At other times, our host and hostess took us to the zoo and to other wonderful places. They had no car, but they and we traveled everywhere by city bus.

We finally received word that we could travel on to New Guinea. What a precious planeload of women and youngsters rose into the air that week in October of 1946! Many hours later, we landed in New Guinea and were reunited with our fathers. Within a few days, we were on the way to Heldsbach, a station on a hill overlooking the Pacific along the Finschhafen coastline. Here Dad proudly escorted us to our new house.

At last we were home!

Else (front right) with parents, Martin & Frieda Helbig; grandparents, Paul & Ernestine Helbig; and siblings, Doris, and Theo.

Else (right) with Simpfendorfer cousins whose family provided refuge for Else's family during World War Two.

two

EMPTY CHAIR AT THE TABLE

Along the ridge of a coral hill dotted with ever-waving coconut palms sat three small army huts, hastily and crudely erected over a slightly sloping slab of concrete. A rusting corrugated iron roof covered the structure. The first building served as a study, where wood shelves of precious books extended to the mottled masonite ceiling. A faintly dank odor emanated from the musty books, some of which had spent 5 long war years hidden underground. The central hut contained a long rectangular table at one end and cane chairs at the other, while a low couch hugged one wall. In the third hut four iron army beds with sagging springs bore lumpy thin mattresses stuffed with kapok. Along one wall stood a large baby bed, fashioned from wood. A narrow rocky path led slightly downhill from the bedroom to the outhouse, a spooky little shack frequented by dangerous wasps and busy spiders.

Several woven grass mats in the house partially covered the ugly gray cement floor, which was erratically peppered with holes and decorated with cracks of varying dimensions. A wooden deck fashioned from hand-hewn timbers led from the center room to a fourth building set apart from the other three: this served as the kitchen. At one end of the kitchen sat a cast iron wood stove, and shelves with crisp feed-sack curtains flanking the walls housed a motley collection of simple dishes and pots and pans. Steps from the kitchen led down to a neatly laid out vegetable garden and offered a breathtaking vista of the Pacific Ocean.

Here was my childhood home.

When I was eight years old, I began having frequent fevers, together with constant pain in my joints; often, too, they felt hot and swollen. I seemed to have no energy whatsoever, and the slightest uphill walks left me dizzy and panting for breath. Even my favorite water hole became impossible to swim across. Our mission doctor diagnosed rheumatic fever, and in those days total bed rest was the common prescription, together with frequent penicillin shots.

My bed hugged the dull green wall adjoining our living room. This wall served as a constant thoroughfare for hundreds of tiny ants which scurried obediently behind a leader like an army of kids playing "Simon Says." On some days the leader ant followed predictable paths, but on other days he veered into fascinating variations of the usual trail, providing endless entertainment for me when I became too ill to read or to sleep.

During the day Mother and Dad carried me to the living room, where the hard narrow couch became my day bed. My folks brought my meals on a colorful tray which became my own mini-table during weeks of illness. I sat propped up in bed to eat, listening to the conversations at table.

Our family was seldom alone during those years. Usually, single teachers ate their meals with us. Some came from the USA, others from Australia, and yet others from Germany. Every meal brought new knowledge and varied conversations. Despite my illness, I wouldn't have missed these conversations for anything in the world. I missed the table a lot; however, I was glad to be able to have everyone nearby, anyway. Many times I felt too weak to eat and I lost much weight. Sometimes when Mother would tuck me into bed and say prayers with me, I would face the wall and pretend to be asleep, and later I would hear her crying softly on her bed. I learned later that neither the doctor nor my folks expected me to live much longer.

Our guests helped to amuse me when they came to visit and to eat. One man sat near my sofa and told stories and legends, punctuating them with dramatic sounds and delightful facial expressions. Another read me stories occasionally, while a couple of the women enjoyed playing Scrabble with me. As a family we sometimes played Chinese checkers or Scrabble together, and we had some favorite card games which were very educational. One was called "Luther's Quartette," a German card game teaching us many basic historical facts about Martin Luther and the Reformation. Another game, called Lotto, was crammed with a cache of fascinating facts about science, inventions, geography, and history. While I was still in bed, my trusty food tray doubled as the main table for our games.

The weekends usually brought additional company. Frequently, one or two members of the hospital staff came for dinner on their day off, and often tourists and folks visiting from other areas for conferences and in-service courses stayed with us. A tiny cottage a short distance up the hill from our house served as the family's guest room. Mother usually roasted a chicken on Sundays, and she made scrumptious gravy to go with the chicken. Our favorite food with chicken was *Spaetzle*, Swabian home-made round noodles made with a little German appliance resembling a potato ricer. For us the chicken gravy over these *Spaetzle* tasted out of this world, and Mother served the dinner with a fresh salad topped with tart homemade salad dressing. Dessert included custard over fresh fruit salad or a freshly baked pineapple meringue pie. No wonder guests regularly appeared for Sunday dinner.

Gradually, I was allowed to move around more and to take part in various activities. I had to take long rests in the afternoons, however, and I spent much of that time reading books and magazines. Our house held many shelves filled with books; I eagerly devoured fascinating stories and novels about distant lands, not realizing that we were actually living in one of those "distant" and "exotic" lands. It was just home to us. Mother subscribed to a women's journal in which sewing patterns came along with each issue. She sewed for the whole family and used these patterns a lot. Whenever the tireless ants could no longer hold my attention during afternoon rest time, I would face the wall and surreptitiously read the love stories in those journals.

As soon as I felt well enough, I was eager to get back to the school books and continue with my correspondence school lessons from Australia. One day, I was permitted to sit at my little desk on the porch again, joining my brother and sister who were also working at their desks.

Most of our food came from the vegetable garden near our home, from fruit trees on the station, and from village women who brought bags of sweet potatoes and vegetables from their food gardens to sell to us. Staple foods such as flour and sugar had to be transported from a supply center, a journey of many hours by boat. Our hot, muggy, rainy weather provided a perfect environment for weevils, so our precious flour frequently became "protein-enriched," dotted with the tiny brown critters. Whenever this happened, we would help Mother on a sunny day by spreading out the contents of a drum of flour over a white sheet, and, sitting around the sheet's perimeter, our friends and we would methodically scoop cupfuls of flour into wire strainers, separating flour from weevils. When the sun was hot enough, the remaining weevils crawled to the edge of the sheet and came to an ignominious end, thanks to us hawk-eyed children. Our stories and jokes, as well as the valuable gossip going around on such days, inevitably turned this otherwise boring activity into a grand social occasion. The only things we hated about those days were the floppy, rimmed cotton hats Mother insisted we wear in the hot sun.

During those years in Finschhafen, village and station families brought their daughters to my mother for training in cooking, cleaning, child-care, and health. Usually, two young indigenous women at a time trained with her, and after a year or two they would marry church workers to whom they'd been engaged. These young women helped our family in many ways and became our good friends, teaching us much about their own culture and language.

Several times a year, sausage-making day provided a variety of chores and entertainment for us children, albeit hot, grueling work for our parents and their helpers. After butchering a pig, they filled tubs full of mysterious-looking chunks of meat. Then they cleaned out the intestines of the pig and boiled them for a long time before they filled them with spiced, ground pork. At regular intervals they tied knots in the intestines, and these chains of sausage links soon went into the big outdoor copper for boiling. We helped by carrying water, chasing flies, and scurrying around singing, laughing, and feigning importance.

After four years of living in this army-hut home, just before I turned eleven, we finally moved into a wonderful, permanent home which Dad and his local carpenters had built for us. We eagerly toted our toys and books across the road and packed them into our new cupboards. My sister Doris and I had a bedroom of our own while our young brother Theo shared a room with my parents. A third bedroom housed guests until Theo needed a room for himself. Again, the center of family and community activities became our table, now a heavy new piece of furniture, waiting for eager life to surround it.

three

MAKE ROOM FOR MORE!

Our family table filled one end of the dining-living room. Three wide windows, framed in green trim, took up most of the wall space at each end of the room. Each window had about twenty green-tinted glass louvers; their tops were perfectly smooth and their undersides were rough, making them a somewhat opaque, but they still admitted lots of light and plenty of air and a fair bit of rain if they weren't tilted at a suitable angle during tropical rainstorms.

Moving this table became a task for two persons, for it was fashioned from sturdy hardwood, complete with a strong wooden brace all the way around and thick wooden legs. Dad had sanded and varnished the table several times, until it glowed with a golden brown finish. During meals we had a cloth on the table, but between meals the table served us in many other ways; for this reason the cloth regularly came off after a meal.

Dad traditionally sat at the end of the table closest to the kitchen, and Mother sat around the corner to his left. That way she could leap up at a moment's notice and scurry into the kitchen for more gravy or salad or for the dessert. Most of the time other people shared meals with us. Doctors, nurses, scientists, preachers, farmers, and students arrived at mealtimes with great regularity and found something to eat. Somehow Mother managed to cook delicious meals for family and company day after day in this place far from any town or supermarket.

The year I turned eleven, 1951, became a year forever etched in my memory. It began with an annual conference for missionaries. More than one hundred missionaries from all over New Guinea arrived in our area of Finschhafen. They held sessions in a large school building, and between sessions my mother, together with several young helpers, provided their meals. During the conference one night we heard strange distant rumblings. They didn't sound like earth tremors, nor was a thunderstorm evident. Dad came home from the sessions and listened to the six o'clock international news on his short-wave radio—a daily ritual which kept him abreast of happenings around the world.

He heard on the radio that Mount Lamington, a volcano about two hundred miles away, was rumbling, but that all people in the area were safe in the event of an eruption. Dad told the assembled dinner guests and family this news as we all sat down to eat. Later, returning for evening sessions, we noticed a big glow in the sky and heard more rumbles. When Dad listened to the ten o'clock news, he learned with horror that the volcano was indeed erupting, and that thousands of villagers were suspected dead. For days we listened to radio broadcasts for more news. The devastation affected thousands of families and food gardens. Whole villages vanished under the deadly, relentless hot lava, and the air currents bore volcanic ash over the whole country and around the world.

As we sat around the table discussing this death and destruction, we felt numb with helplessness. I looked out of the windows at the blue, jungle-covered mountains behind our house, wondering whether one of them was also a volcano. I tried to imagine how we would run away from an eruption, or how safe it would be to leap into the ocean. Dad had told us about a great earthquake which he'd experienced and which had set off a huge, destructive tidal wave in the ocean, and suddenly the thought of fleeing into the sea lost its attraction for me.

Fear piled upon fear that January, as I had to enter our local hospital soon after the volcano's eruption. Our doctor decided that my tonsils, perhaps through a streptococcal infection following a bad case of the measles, had caused my earlier attack of rheumatic fever. Moreover, the fevers and sore throats seemed to be never-ending. He decreed that it was time to remove the tonsils. The hospital consisted of a crudely converted row of army quarters left over from World War Two, and I remember lying on a squeaky, iron-framed bed with a gas mask over my face. The sickly-sweet smell of the gas remains seared in my memory, and I vividly recall the eeriest dreams I had during the surgery.

After several days in the hospital, I was glad to come home and to sit at our normal table once again, with my family members plus a few unfamiliar guests. My somewhat limited diet didn't stop me from listening and actively joining in with the conversations at meal times.

In February I had to prepare for yet another new fear, namely, that of leaving home. Mother tried to be cheerful those weeks, but I detected some apprehension and sadness, and I knew she was trying to cope with the thought of sending me far away to school. After years of correspondence lessons under Mother's capable supervision, I was to go to a "real" school in order to be better prepared for secondary school later on. Mother sewed some new garments for me on her treadle sewing machine, and I helped with hemming and ironing. Together we collected and packed my belongings into a suitcase.

A few weeks later, I left by boat and then by airplane for a totally strange destination called Wau, a quaint gold-mining town hugging steep, pine-covered hillsides within a large, picturesque valley. Here the new school for missionaries' children was ready, though not yet completed, for its first, unsure occupants. A number of us children who were going to this school knew one another quite well; this helped to make the wrenching from family a bit easier. For us the thought of being pioneer students at a newly built school fueled our thrills for dramatic events in life, and we managed to cook up all kinds of adventures in the dormitory during those first months. Nights, however, were often fear-filled and sleepless for me, accompanied by mysterious sounds from outside and waves of homesickness.

While we adjusted to dormitory life and new foods as well as new teachers and classes, carpenters were busy completing the plumbing and indoor bathrooms during the first weeks of school. We had to use sturdy outhouses behind the dormitory. One chilly night, my roommate and I had to obey a call of nature and make a visit outdoors. I was proudly carrying my red flashlight, a parting gift from my father. With our teeth chattering, both from fear and from cold, we bundled up in our flannel dressing gowns and slipped outside. I clutched my flashlight as we trudged to the outhouse, and I went in and sat down. Suddenly a sickening thud and splash confirmed my worst fear: my flashlight had slipped off my lap and had fallen many feet into the depths of the latrine. I jumped up and dashed out, crying hysterically. My roommate tried to comfort me while feeling her way into the building and completing her ablutions; then we hurriedly padded back to the dormitory in the dark, starless night.

Slowly, we grew to enjoy our new surroundings at Wau. We loved exploring the forest paths and hillsides during the weekends. We lived for mail day, and whenever we heard the whine of a tiny single-engine aircraft over the distant hills, we trembled with excitement and hope for mail from home. I enjoyed mealtimes at Wau, but I really missed my mealtimes together with my own family. To be sure, we had good food at the school, and we had an excellent staff-student ratio for caring and personal attention, but at first we felt our house parents were strangers, and we just couldn't relax at mealtimes. We soon got to know one another very well, however, and we had some marvelous times together. I still keep up with some of the friendships I made there more than five decades ago.

One night a teacher came to the dormitory to tell me that my Aunt Clara, who had served with my Uncle Georg along New Guinea's northern coast, had died suddenly after unexpected surgery near Madang. *Not more death, please, God, not more death*, was all I could think. This death came much closer to our family than those from the distant volcano. It struck terror in my imagination as I tried to imagine my own mother's death.

At the same time, the illnesses of my early childhood resurfaced to cause me many days of fevers and joint pains. After several weeks of pain and fever, the doctor advised me to return home, where I spent many more weeks in bed with another attack of rheumatic fever.

Although I missed my friends at school, I did not mind being in the middle of the action at home again, where never a dull moment existed, even for a bedridden child. Our wide windows, open porch, daily radio broadcasts, and a constant stream of guests provided endless stimulation—perhaps at times too much. During the weeks when I was too weak to sit at the table, Mother would prepare a tray of food which I ate propped up in bed. She kept the door wide open, so that I could hear everything and interject now and then with a comment. The metal tray with its now somewhat faded hand-painted picture of flowers again became my own tiny table for many weeks.

During December of 1951, my widowed uncle and four motherless cousins came to spend the Christmas vacation with our family. The ten of us managed to fit around the dining room table. These mealtimes provided interesting challenges for our parents, for our cousins' upbringing had been very different from ours. Soon we got to know one another better, however, and mealtimes became happily punctuated with wild school stories mixed with much teasing, arguing, and joking.

Our big kitchen seldom sat idle, for cooking and baking took up a lot of time for our family living a hundred miles by ship from the nearest town. Every few months, staple foods such as flour and sugar and canned goods would arrive by boat; fresh vegetables and fruit, sweet potatoes and taro, fresh eggs and pork came locally—either from our own yard and garden, or from the surrounding villages.

Little did we dream that my uncle would also die before the following Christmas vacation. Suddenly, my parents had the serious responsibility for not only three children but also four more. Our nuclear family constellation changed forever as the children from two very differing family environments merged into one family unit. That previous Christmas the stage had been set for a blended family. Now Kate, Walter, Traude, and Anne, burdened and puzzled by the deaths of both of their parents within such a short time, bravely joined our family and began to rebuild their shattered lives around a new table, a table with different rules and with different foods, but one filled with love and community. Their and our frustrations over widely differing worldviews often bubbled to the surface during mealtimes, but we gained valuable practice in mediation and in developing relationships. My quiet, deeply meditative father, who often fell ill with asthma, and my vivacious mother with her incredibly huge heart for love and tolerance despite her health restrictions as an insulin-dependent diabetic, together built some middle ground in which to continue to nurture their brood of now seven youngsters. As different as my parents' personalities were, they nevertheless demonstrated a valuable capacity to talk things over together, even when they did not see eye to eye about something.

They taught us many precious lessons for life. Sure, at times Dad became upset or Mother had tears in her eyes when she came to the table, but by the next meal she was her bubbly self again, and we knew she and Dad had talked things over.

Christmas Eve was the highpoint of our vacation times. Coming home from boarding school, we'd been squirreling away various bits of fabric or paint or wood or embroidery thread to create gifts for one another. Some of us brought home gifts we'd made at school, and we had to hide them in a safe place until December 24th—not a simple procedure in a three-bedroom house overrun by nine persons for those weeks. Inevitably, someone discovered a hidden gift on a shelf; accusations of "snooping" ensued. The boys spent hours down in Dad's little tool shed, building breadboards or candle holders or vase holders. I still have a wooden vase holder my brother carved for me by creating a lacy pattern of scores of meticulously cut holes with his tiny, hand-powered jig-saw.

Christmas baking times were special. We gathered around the big table armed with knives, colored frosting, and large trays. We'd baked lots of cutout cookies the previous day, and now we were ready to apply our talents to decorating the cookies. Two of the girls were fastidious about decorating while the rest of us slapped on the frosting carelessly, joking, narrating, and teasing, making sure enough frosting would regularly drop for us to sample. When we almost reached the end of the frosting, we mixed the last bits together in one bowl, attaining a sickening dark gray hue, and we then proceeded to cover a few last cookies with this goop.

We did not put gifts under the tree. Instead, my parents dragged the heavy dining table into the center of the room. They added another table and covered both with a huge white cloth. Without fail, others joined our already big family for Christmas celebrations, for Mother never wanted anyone to be without family at Christmas. Singles, young couples, and new families often joined us at these times. We busily embroidered their monograms onto plain handkerchiefs that we girls had sewn, and we added a carving or a trinket or a box of home-baked cookies for each guest. At dusk on Christmas Eve we carried home-baked rolls and decorated cookies to our neighbors and friends. After that, we were ready to focus on the celebrations.

The evening began with a simple supper, followed by a long church service at the nearby church. Hundreds of people came from villages all around to take part in the Christmas nativity drama and worship. Often, the drama involved sheeted shepherds, two-legged human sheep creeping up the center of the church aisles on all fours, “bleating” loudly, and a simple manger in a thatched roof stable in front of the church. Sometimes the drama took place outdoors in the dark, where burning coconut leaf torches, swaying in the sturdy brown hands of rhythmic dancers, provided intermittent lighting as the drama unfolded.

Finally, the service ended, and our flashlights bobbed as we scurried home over the rocky coral road to the house, bursting with eagerness to get on with our own celebrations. Mother and Dad hurried home to cover the table with gifts, and we children scurried to our rooms, reaching high and deep into shelves and drawers to unearth the gifts we had been hiding. We handed my folks these mysterious lumps of packages that they placed in the designated positions. At the sound of a tinkling bell from the Christmas tree, we all trooped in solemnly, and our parents showed us where to sit. Each of us found a pile of gifts, and down the center of the table sat trays of goodies flanked by gorgeous hibiscus blossoms nested amid delicate green wisps of fern. We began our family Christmas ceremony with Christmas carols and prayers of thanks, and then we were allowed to open packages. Meanwhile, we took turns jumping up to pass around the goodies, or to refill our glasses of juice, and to hilariously recall previous Christmas times together.

Even on that first uncertain Christmas as a family of nine, when we were still numb with the horror and mystery of two recent deaths, and when tears often welled up in our eyes as we sat around the table to say grace before our meals, we knew we were on the way to establishing special bonds as a new family.

four

"ALL WE EVER GET IS OATMEAL"

A few years ago, my seven-year-old daughter, clad in a dirty gray-brown smock, made her acting debut by leading the orphan chorus onto stage for the poignant opening number of the musical "Oliver." I sat in the audience on the edge of my chair, and when she came into view, followed by plaintive, somber-faced youngsters carrying their pitiful bowls and sang the line, "All we ever get is gruel," my eyes welled up with tears. My memory went back to St. Peters, where I would try to eat oatmeal for breakfast every morning. My throat thickened and my eyes shut as I tried to swallow the lumpy oatmeal that was probably a generous donation from some kind farmer who wanted to do something for the church. It's hardly fair for me to compare our lives with that of Oliver, for Oliver and his band of orphans suffered real hardships and real hunger, whereas we at St. Peters merely had unpleasant-tasting food that we could always supplement with white bread. Yet, for me, a host of memories surfaced, taking me back to my high school years.

While a harsh gong sounded in the distance, hundreds of teenagers thronged out of their classrooms, heading for the long low dining hall to get their food for lunch. Girls wore pleated maroon smocks over crisp, and sometimes not-so-crisp, white blouses. In winter they also wore maroon felt ties bound around their necks. White socks and black tied shoes completed the uniform for everyday wear, but whenever they left campus, they also had to wear wide-brimmed straw hats. Boys wore blue shirts with maroon-colored trim, and for dress-up as well as for winter, they wore ties, too.

This beautiful campus, set amid stately gum trees and many other trees and shrubs on rolling hills in the semi-tropical city of Brisbane in Australia, became home for my four years of secondary school education. Our formal education took place in crowded classrooms within a two-floor block of buildings. The upper floor served as a chapel and assembly hall, while the lower floor housed classrooms, offices, and a small library, the doorway to fascinating worlds of knowledge for me.

St. Peter's, in the nineteen fifties, had the distinction of being one of the few private secondary coeducational schools in Australia. School rules forbade us from mixing with persons of the opposite sex, unless the other person happened to be a sibling. After chapel every evening, siblings were permitted to meet for a few minutes in a designated spot on the cement apron at the bottom of the chapel steps. Inevitably, we gained some interesting new "siblings" at such times, and we often managed to persuade our real siblings to bring along an "adopted" brother or sister with whom we wished to become better acquainted. This worked only for a few minutes, however, since a supervising teacher would soon snoop around and banish the imposter from the designated family spot.

We found interesting ways to build relationships with forbidden students. We could steal glances at one another whenever the teacher was writing on the board. Also, we could write notes in mirror language to one another, passing them under desks across the classroom with trusted persons. The recipient decoded the message by holding up the notes near a mirror. Sometimes, this method was too public, however, and one ran the risk of being teased on campus some time later that week. A third way we could have some stolen moments of visiting together was an arrangement to make an appointment with the dentist or doctor off campus on the same afternoon and accidentally meet and walk together along the little backwoods shortcut which led to the commercial center. Again, this involved risks, since teachers often found excuses to go to the shopping area, too, and they kept their eyes wide open wherever they went.

Mealtimes were segregated affairs, since the boys sat on tables down one side of the long dining hall and girls sat on tables down the other side. For at least one meal a day, a teacher sat at the head of every table. In the center of the line of boys' tables perched a staff table, bristling with vigilant teachers under the leadership of our principal, who often threw his head back to scan the whole dining room during the meal.

We received assigned places at the tables, and every week we would rotate our places at that same table. Menus became very predictable, for often the same dishes were served on the same night each week. Breakfasts usually consisted of cooked oatmeal or cooked cream of wheat. As a change from oatmeal, some mornings we had "fry-up," a mushy mixture of reheated mashed pumpkin and potatoes from a previous meal. Actually, this tasted quite good, and we could eat it over slices of white bread. At lunchtime, we made boring sandwiches from white bread with a choice of "fingernail polish,"—the name we assigned to a kind of plum jam which arrived daily at the table—marmalade, and Vegemite. How we envied the children of our sister college in the southern city of Adelaide, because they received fresh fruit some days and actually had a choice of apricot jam or marmalade for their bread. For me the worst meal came on Thursday nights, when we had to eat tripe. Countless times I almost gagged on this dish, and my knowledge that it came from the lining of a cow's stomach did nothing to lessen my abhorrence for this food.

Sundays often became days of homesickness, and Sunday's menu, offered soon after morning chapel finished, did little to assuage our yearning for a home-cooked Sunday dinner. We girls trooped into the dining hall in our white Sunday dresses and brown shoes. Sunday's menu often included wilted shredded lettuce, boiled potatoes, and a kind of rolled roast beef, cooked ahead of time and then sliced cold and served. Every mouthful yielded snippets of string which had been tied around the meat, and we spent the meal dislodging this string from our plates and from between our teeth. I sat at the table on Sundays and dreamed of Sunday dinner at home, with roast chicken and gravy over the wonderful German noodles called *Spaetzle,* flanked by a crisp salad. Fortunately, dessert tasted quite good on Sundays, for we often had custard with canned fruit.

In spite of our monotonous diet, I have happy memories of many of our table times together. I have often asked myself how that could possibly be. Here in a place where the word "choice" barely existed in our vocabulary, neither for food nor for roommates, we nevertheless had a choice of friends and discussion topics. Our predictable meals furnished us with shared misery as well as shared joy and bonded us, as we eagerly discussed school and family, teased one another about boys, and cried when a hurtful remark or a sharp reprimand shattered our fragile self-esteem. Moreover, clustered closely around the tables, we tested our conversational skills, practiced mediation techniques, and gossiped endlessly about teachers and housemothers. Here, we grew out of awkward, innocent childhood into realistic young adulthood.

Occasionally, we entertained ourselves at mealtimes by sponsoring an eating competition. Word spread that "Pete" would participate in an eating contest, and that if we wanted to support the idea, we should pass all our spare bread to his table and he would try to consume it. Several other tables chose a hero likewise, and each table of boys participating in the contest would appoint one trustworthy young man to keep accurate count. At the sound of the dinner gong, we lined up obediently in front of the dining hall, quivering with anticipation and anxious to get inside. However, the prefect in charge at the head of the line waited until we were all orderly and silent before she motioned us to begin marching indoors.

We marched in and scrambled to our assigned places, bowing for the table grace and hastily surveying the food. We ate a minimum of bread and silently passed the rest of it to Pete's table. Letting the slices of bread cross the median of the dining hall to the boys' side represented no mean feat, for ever-watchful teachers could detect trouble even if they couldn't see it. Pete, meantime, gobbled down one slice of bread after another, lubricating it with smidgens of butter and little slabs of jam. He washed the bread down with hot brown sweetened tea from a big iron teapot on the table, and when that ran out, friends from other tables passed more tea across to his table.

Whenever the principal rose for the closing prayer, everyone had to rise with him, and the meal was officially over, whether we were finished or not. This night, the principal was rising. Pete had to stop eating. His mouth still stuffed, he rose heavily and gobbled down the last slice of bread during grace. We dashed out the door, and the word got around that he won the contest by consuming 21 slices of bread. Needless to say, he wasn't feeling very well in the afternoon, but he was a good-natured young man and he survived.

Not long after this, some of the fellows ran a new contest, and this involved drinking cupfuls of tea. Again, admirers and assistants passed on their tea, and by the end of the meal the winner had consumed seventeen cupfuls of tea.

When Pete, enthusiastic over a whole slew of new admirers from the girls' side of the dining hall, volunteered to eat a spider for a price, we drew the line. Not to be taken aback, Pete found a person on the boys' side willing to part with some money, and the spider-eating contest took place out of sight from us squeamish womenfolk.

Secret midnight feasts occasionally took place toward the end of a school year and involved meticulous, surreptitious, planning. First, we had to set a date for the feast. Next, we had to decide who would come to the feast. Moreover, we had to plan the menu and the shopping. We had to begin buying the food downtown when we were going for another reason. Finally, we had to designate a suitably scary place reasonably out of earshot from the house mother—either in a dormitory building or out in the woods behind the dormitory. I opted for the dorm, because the woods held frightening sounds and creatures for me. Nights were sometimes scary enough even in the dormitories, for our windows weren't screened; consequently, little bugs occasionally flew in and frightened me. Worse, an eerie chattering sometimes wakened me, rendering me to a trembling mass beneath my covers. I would then discover the silhouette of an opossum on the windowsill, screeching at us. My mosquito net tucked under my mattress around me was small solace for me, for I knew a puny mosquito net could not hold back a creature so large, especially one with claws. In spite of many fear-filled nights, I did not once have an opossum jump on my bed or attack me in any way; however, I imagined such an attack a thousand times!

Slowly, details of our little feast developed, but by the designated night I felt very guilty and not at all keen to go through with our plan. On one hand, I was excited about being invited by my good friends to the party. On the other hand, I doubted I'd have the courage to carry through with such a daring defiance of the school's rules. At last the night arrived. We went to bed at the correct time and wakened one another a few hours later. We stole outdoors (my friends had outvoted me regarding the venue), lugging our goodies, and the crunching sounds of our tiptoed feet padding down the wooded path sent shivers of fear down our spines. Mysterious forest sounds magnified in the starless night. Finally, we reached the hiding place, sat down in a circle, and began to eat. We stuffed ourselves with mouthwatering fruit salad, cream cookies, and other succulent foods, giggling nervously and waiting for a wild animal or a staff member to pounce on us and grab us by the collar at any moment.

Back: Traude, Kate, Walter, Else. Front: Theo, Doris, Anne
We all attended St. Peter's College for secondary schooling.

To our surprise, no uninvited guests arrived. Feeling more than satisfied and slightly queasy, we shuffled back to our dormitory, scattered to our rooms, climbed back into bed, and lay wide-awake for a long time. Next morning, our house mother acted in a strange way and seemed a bit short-tempered with me, and I wondered whether and how she found out about our secret feast. I surmised that my guilty conscience was so obvious, that she didn't have to ask any questions nor actually see anything unusual happen.

Thus another year passed at St. Peters, and on "break-up" day we eagerly caught taxis to the airport and clambered aboard an airplane for home and family in New Guinea.

five

TEA FOR TEN

Our wide-open porch ran along the eastern front and almost the whole northern side of our green-trimmed tropical home. On sultry days every breath of wind felt like a refreshing, soothing balm. On rainy days I leaned on the rounded wood railing and watched as rain pelted down in massive sheets, engulfing our house and pounding the iron roof. During stormy nights the porch offered a panorama of forked lightning streaking the sky for wild instants, resembling some heart monitor machine gone awry.

Northwards, smoky-blue mountains towered to greet the sky, and all around the house stood lush green shrubs and trees, frequented by colorful birds such as regal blue kingfishers, fluorescent green parakeets, tiny golden hummingbirds, and snowy cockatoos, their somewhat discordant symphony providing background music for our daily activities. Among gently nodding hibiscus blooms darted the silent ones—gorgeous butterflies in flashes of azure, emerald, black, and gold. A red clambering rose bush hugged the porch rails, its sweet fragrance borne for brief moments along little gusts of air.

My favorite porch view faced the east, where lay an infinite expanse of the vast Pacific, shimmering blue on sunny days, rolling and frothing on windy days, and pouring in gray sheets on rainy days, mysteriously merging with the distant horizon. After a night of heavy rains, our flooded river spewed out its muddy overflow, forming large brown stains that spread and blended with the blue sea in ever-widening arcs, creating a variegation of brown, green, aqua, and blue stripes. At night the golden moon slid gently upwards from the sea, throwing a wide, glistening bridge across the water for some moments, then hiding behind woolly clouds and obscuring the bridge.

Our porch formed an essential, integral part of our very existence. Near the railing the younger children sat at small wooden tables, toiling daily at correspondence school lessons. Alongside the guest room door stood Mother's ancient, ever dependable treadle sewing machine, churning out colorful clothing for the family. In one corner, on a musty old trunk from days gone by, stood our sturdy dollhouse, fashioned by Dad from wooden crates, its rough edges covered with tiny, soft curtains.

The hub of the porch, however, was at the northeast corner—our center for times together, and our refuge for times alone. In those rickety woven cane chairs we sat and talked, argued, loved, laughed, and wept together. There we met new friends and shared with old ones. There we girls stole smiling glances at visiting boys, and, when the older members of the family went inside, we sat and discussed the deeper matters of life with them.

For many months of the year, those of us who were in high school and university in Australia were far away from home. When the (summer) Christmas vacation rolled around, we eagerly returned home to New Guinea, if we and our families could afford it, and the family suddenly grew very large again. Saturday afternoon tea on the porch was the weekend special, and guests inevitably joined us at that time. For such occasions the round wicker table wore a hand-embroidered cloth, its center graced with a vase full of blossoms from the garden—a few orchids among fragile, green fern, some exotic hibiscus, delicate nodding gerberas, or a cluster of scented roses. Cups and saucers arrived from the kitchen, clattering precariously in my eager hands. Soon Mother carried out a platter laden with scrumptious home-baked yeast rolls, whose irresistible aroma had permeated the house for hours. Bursting with cinnamon, sugar, and raisins, with frosting trickling deliciously from their tops, these rolls sat invitingly on the table. Between mouthfuls we laughed and talked, and in that rare moment when nobody spoke and even the birds were silent, I thrilled to the distant crash of restless waves breaking over the rocky shoreline half a mile away.

Only a dire emergency interrupted this Saturday ritual. However, we never became bored, for every week the cast varied. Sometimes we hosted neighbors who were my parents' teaching colleagues. Sometimes the doctor's family or a couple of nurses from the nearby hospital came for their afternoon off. Whenever this happened, we teenagers learned all kinds of medical terminology while listening to hair-raising accounts of medical crises. At other times travelers from far-off lands came "to study a primitive country" and, to our chagrin, claimed to become instant experts about the land as soon as they returned to their home countries. Anthropologists, entomologists, church dignitaries, medical researchers, and linguists represented just a smattering of the experts who joined us for tea and goodies on the porch. To be sure, some were wonderful guests, open-minded, and eager to engage in true dialogue with us. Others had their minds made up before they even set foot in the country, and we'd exchange secret, knowing glances as soon as they began spouting off their academic solutions for the country's problems.

We chuckled later while impersonating some of our more unwelcome guests, but whenever we did this, our parents gently reminded us of other sides to such persons, suggesting that there may have been a perfectly good reason for one person's attitude or words. They encouraged us to ask astute questions and to listen carefully for the answers before we made up our minds about people.

One by one, we children left the security of home for school in Australia and for life in the big world. One by one, we wrenched ourselves away from the family table indoors and from the nostalgic porch outdoors. At the end of the school year, we returned for summer vacation, and nothing quite matched the excitement of walking up the steps onto the porch, dragging suitcases and hand bags, dropping them at the top of the steps, drinking in a deliciously deep breath of fresh ocean air, and throwing up our arms to take it all in: the restless, shimmering ocean, bordered by tall green coconut palms; our brown neighbors stopping to greet us while ambling along the coral pathway past our house; the lusciously green shrubs and liana tendrils flanking the porch; and, best of all, the family gathering to greet us.

When I turned nineteen, I came home from the University of Queensland in Australia for vacation after a two-year absence. My excitement at coming back to the familiar house and porch knew no bounds, and I dashed up the steps as fast as I could, dragging my luggage, depositing it, and then looking around. The family included a tall young red-haired man who looked quite unfamiliar. I'd heard about him, as he had been teaching with my father, and his name was Ron.

Ron and I became acquainted fast through many visits on the porch as well as many discussions while taking walks, going swimming, and singing together around the pump organ indoors. I suddenly wanted to bake cakes and cookies for Saturday teas; moreover, I became intensely interested in studying recipe books. In the evenings we sat around the tiny wicker table in the creaky cane chairs, inhaling the breathtaking view of an enormous silvery moon-ball rising out of the dark sea.

One night, Ron asked whether I would consider becoming his partner for life. Awed and a little uncertain, somewhat fearful of the vast unknown future, which would possibly include moving to the United States of America, I answered with a tentative, "Perhaps." Soon this reply changed into a definite "Yes!" and our discussions around the circular wicker table on the porch included much serious planning for the months to come.

After Ron completed his two years of volunteer service in New Guinea in 1960, both as a carpenter and a teacher, he returned to the United States to finish his university degree and enroll at Wartburg Seminary in Dubuque, Iowa, for theological studies. Meanwhile, I returned to Australia for two more years of study at the University of Queensland to complete my Bachelor of Arts degree and a Diploma in Education. During those two years we made many plans by writing letters, and I applied to emigrate from Australia to the USA. Finally, in May of 1962 I boarded a ship for many great unknowns: four weeks of travel on the high seas to reach the USA; a reunion with Ron whom I hadn't seen for two years; a wedding I'd helped plan from ten thousand miles away, without the convenience of phone calls or e-mail; and a contract to teach high school German and Mathematics in a new land.

Afternoon tea with the Helbig family at Heldsbach, Finschhafen

A gathering of missionaries and volunteers at Finschhafen

six

HONEYMOON HOME

We moved into a snug mobile home in Dubuque, Iowa in the United States after our wedding in July of 1962. Barely twenty-four feet long and eight feet wide, our home nestled on a hillside of Wartburg Seminary's trailer court together with thirty-five other homes of varying lengths and widths.

This nifty cubby house, our very own honeymoon quarters, provided shelter, warmth, and bliss as we began our married life together. Sometimes I had to pinch myself to see that all of this was real. I admired the tiny wooden cabinets that formed excellent storage nooks. A narrow cupboard door opened to reveal a tiny bathroom ensemble, complete with shower stall, small sink, and compact toilet. In addition, these conveniences were just one and a half steps from the bed, which entirely filled our bedroom at one end of our home. A two-drawer cabinet at our feet held our underwear and socks, and three years later, its flat, narrow top served as a perfect shelf to hold a baby bassinet.

Here we had a kitchen where we could reach every cabinet or appliance without taking a step forward or backward. We crammed our precious wedding gifts into the narrow cabinets and used them day after day.

Our living room held a sofa opening out into a full bed, thus doubling as our spare room for guests. Between kitchen and sofa stood a square foldout table, and this tiny table became our food and fellowship and office center. Here we sat and ate our meals. Some were quite delicious, while others were somewhat charred outcomes of new culinary experiments by the unskilled bride. Every evening I spread my Mathematics and German textbooks over the table and pored over them for hours, preparing my lessons to teach at the high school the next day. Between lesson-planning sessions I would sit with my elbows propped on the wobbly table, staring out through our gorgeous picture window, trying to figure out effective ways to teach Calculus and difficult word problems in Algebra.

Every week I wrote letters to my parents and family, who were scattered in Australia and Papua New Guinea; we both wrote to Ron's folks, Martha and Arthur Schardt, who lived in Nebraska at the time. Although Ron had a study desk in one of the dormitories at the seminary, he sometimes brought home books later in the evening in order to be at home when it became late. Fitting two lots of study books on the table took a bit of maneuvering and cooperation. To my delight, our elbows often touched across the little corner!

Directly above our table, just under the golden plywood ceiling of our mobile home, nestled a golden-brown cabinet adorned with glass doors. Carved borders surrounded the glass, and we liked this decorative touch. This cabinet housed our record player, and, especially on Saturdays, I often had the hi-fi going while cleaning house. Even now, decades later, we still have a few of those records, and whenever I play them, I can picture the trailer home and its pretty cabinets. My favorite records at that time were one of Strauss Waltzes and one called "Classical Music For People Who Don't Know Anything About Classical Music."

Our collapsible table became a sewing center during vacation times, for we had received a wonderfully practical, Singer featherweight sewing machine as a gift from Ron's parents. The machine ran its first miles of stitching during our time in the mobile home.

One of the first Saturdays after our wedding, Ron began to clear the table and spread some newspapers over it. Baking in the kitchen nook and wondering what was coming, I was surprised to see him drag a big toolbox out from under the trailer. He opened it and began to lay various tools on the table.

"That's my table. What are you doing with that stuff on my table?" I wailed.

"This table is also my table," he calmly replied, "Where else do you think I can build?"

"But you will mess up the house," I protested, "Your tools will be dirty. You will make dust if you saw."

"Remember, you wanted me to fix some things and build some things," he reminded me. I sighed and capitulated, covering the sofa and other precious items with sheets whenever the "workshop" was in session. How that rickety table ever survived so many unintended functions amazed me.

One morning, someone knocked on the door—a classmate of Ron, asking for his regular hair trim. Ron brought out the clippers and spread them on the table. His friend, who hailed from a Nebraska farm, was easily six feet five inches tall. He stooped carefully as he stepped into our parlor and eased himself into one of our two chairs. His knees were too high to fit under the table, so he simply stretched them out toward the door, totally blocking access from any direction. After that haircut the two men decided to cut hair up in the central house, a cold old building in the middle of our mobile home court; it housed showers and toilets for those persons whose homes did not come with such conveniences, as well as sturdy Maytag washing machines for the residents to use.

Not long after this, our tall friend and his tall wife became our first dinner guests. We hoped all four of us would actually fit into the room somehow. I spent hours preparing a good Australian chicken curry and fixing a special dessert we would eat with my silver cake forks; they'd been an engagement gift from Australian friends. We unfolded the extra flap of the table and spread our little Chinese embroidered tablecloth over it. Out came the wedding gift plates and stainless flatware and glasses. I bustled about at the stove, stirring, tasting, fussing, and eagerly waiting to serve the food.

Dinnertime came, and our guests arrived. They graciously ate, and together we visited and laughed and joked. They said they liked the food. At dessert time I put dessert on the plates, flanked them with silver forks, and passed them around. The dessert was a success, but our tall friend had such big hands that he found no way to hold my dainty cake fork and use it to eat the dessert. We often laughed about this in later years.

These guests were the first of many who delighted us by accepting invitations to eat in our humble cubby house. Whenever we couldn't fit around the table, we spilled over onto the sofa, and if that filled up, too, we kept the door open and sat a couple of people in the doorway. Naturally, this became impossible during the cold winter months, but during winter we did not entertain as much either, as those were times of intense study and lesson planning. Special events included visits by Ron's folks and his aunt and uncle; also, my cousin Mary, a doctor from Australia, made a visit in the middle of a cold winter. We had a splendid time together those days, reminiscing, catching up on one another's news, showing her around historical Dubuque, and trying hard to keep warm whenever we stepped outdoors.

We have lived in many types of houses since those precious first years in our tiny mobile home. Some had large dining rooms, some had large kitchens, and one had a very tiny kitchen nook almost the same size as our mobile home kitchen. But never has the size of the table or the house hindered us from inviting people to come and share table fellowship with us. As long as we found a bit of table space on which to set some food, we enjoyed sharing this space with others.

In 1965, after Ron graduated from the seminary, we were called to serve as missionaries in New Guinea. Together with our new-born daughter, Joy, we once again traversed the vast Pacific by ship, not separately this time but as a happy family of three, to begin new adventures in a land we had grown to love in the past.

seven

PRESSURE POINTS

The Finisterre Range towers raggedly and formidably behind the northeastern coastline of Papua New Guinea. Tapen, situated at an altitude of five thousand feet above sea level on one of the range's foothills, offers a magnificent panoramic view of the blue, blue Pacific, complete with a pair of volcanic islands on the horizon. Dawn over the ocean provides a daily festival, beginning with rosy hints of light on the horizon, turning brighter orange with every minute, and breaking suddenly into an explosion of brilliance as the giant orb of sun rises out of the sea. Within two hours, huge cotton balls of fog sail in from below, banishing the short-lived sunlight, and permeating the whole village. Nothing blocks the advance of this fog. Often such tufts of fog sail right through open windows of our house, across the living room, and out through the opposite windows.

Tapen, our home for fifteen brief, life-changing months, had two entryways from the outside world. One was a forty-minute flight by light aircraft from Madang, our supply base and nearest town. Only one airplane in the country could land at Tapen—a small STOL (Short Take-Off and Landing) Cessna aircraft, as the airstrip was a mere eight hundred feet long and had a twelve percent slope. Some years earlier the villagers had performed an incredible feat by carving that airstrip out of the mountainside by hand, using spades and wheelbarrows over many back-breaking months of work. Aircraft transported coffee to town—the only cash crop or source of income for the villagers in that area. In addition, medical supplies, kerosene for lamps, and other goods were flown in at great expense to the people. The airplane brought precious mail and supplies, and it also helped transport evangelists to other remote areas as well as critically ill patients to the hospital in Madang.

The second entryway from "outside" involved catching a coastal boat to the seaside village of Malalamai, then walking straight uphill for six hours, until one reached Tapen. Villagers from further inland reached Tapen by climbing incredibly rugged mountain ranges, nimbly scaling a four-hour sheer mountainside before reaching the station.

Tapen became a wonderful place for language study, because hardly anyone there spoke English. We eagerly threw ourselves into learning the Kotte language, and we constantly had willing helpers among our New Guinean coworkers, who spoke slowly for our sakes and who patiently corrected our mispronunciations, until we became more confident with the language. Never will we forget our neighbors in Tapen, who so lovingly welcomed us white strangers and forgave us our mispronunciations and faltering questions about their culture.

I dreamed of helping these people with their education and of helping the teachers in the schools. After all, very few of the people in that area could read or write. Soon after we moved there, however, many desperately ill and ailing people came to our door, some dripping with huge tropical ulcers, others weakened by intestinal diseases, and yet others emaciated and hollow with tuberculosis, pneumonia, or malaria.

I was horrified. I was a teacher, not a doctor, and yet these people needed help, and there was no one else to help them. My fear of treating someone wrongly rivaled my aversion to sores, blood, and dangerous illnesses. *What if one of us catches something? What if our baby daughter gets ill?* These became daily, haunting questions for me.

Often reaching for the medicine cabinet, I carefully read instructions and called the hospital on the radio-transceiver whenever necessary. A nurse at the hospital many miles away in Madang relayed my descriptions to the doctor, who then prescribed the necessary medication. At my desperate plea for help, a nurse friend from the United States airmailed me the latest edition of the Merck Manual, and that became my Bible for diagnosing illnesses. I took a while to understand the technical language of the Merck, finding it somewhat like studying yet another language. Our trusty Webster's Collegiate Dictionary was not, after all, a medical dictionary; however, I soon found the Merck an invaluable aid for describing the symptoms of various illnesses.

On Easter Saturday of 1967, while we sat at breakfast, we heard some noises outside. I went out and saw a thin young stranger limping awkwardly down the hill toward our house. He sagged down onto the grass in our yard before he reached the house, gasping in short, weakened breaths. His eyes rolled, and he was clutching his leg. A tourniquet made from long leaves and jungle vines circled his upper leg, while a blood-soaked wad of bunched leaves surrounded his toes. I knelt down beside him and began to remove the tourniquet, gently telling him we needed to take it off. He protested feebly, fearful of more bleeding. I raised his leg high and removed the blood-matted covers from the wound on his foot. The wound was right between his first and second toes, and blood began to spurt up again.

We applied pressure directly to the wound and clumsily carried the young man to our house, made him comfortable, and elevated his foot. Meanwhile, we tried calling a doctor on the radio transceiver, as the young man had obviously lost an awful lot of blood. Also, he was running a fever and he needed to get to hospital. The doctor alerted our mission pilot in Madang, and within a couple of hours he radioed back to say the aircraft was on the way. Limp with relief, we began the wait for it while taking turns applying pressure to the wound to stem the bleeding.

One hour passed, then two, then three, and we heard the roar of a plane overhead. By this time we were totally engulfed by thick billowing fog and damp, grey clouds which literally hugged the mountaintops, the treetops, and the ground. Our pilot tried in vain to find a hole in the clouds, and finally he radioed to say that he was sorry but he could not try anymore today, and that he would try again early on Monday morning.

I was incredulous. "Monday? Did he say Monday? But this is Saturday! How can we wait until Monday? What am I going to do with this guy dying in my house?" I went off to the bedroom and had a good cry while someone else held Mainao's foot. We radioed the doctor again, and he suggested that I try to sew up the blood vein. I almost passed out just thinking about that. We found a rounded suture needle and some catgut that was ideal for tough skin but far too thick for something as delicate as a blood vessel. Meanwhile, our patient was running a fever of 104 degrees F., so the doctor also instructed me to inject large doses of penicillin every four hours. That was another skill I'd never learned in education courses at the university. In the absence of a local anesthetic, we tried to administer some phenol-barbital to try to make our patient sleepier, but he remained very alert while lying quietly without wincing when I jabbed him.

My attempt at suturing the blood vessel was a total failure. I reeled with nausea and fear every time I tried, for the thread was just too coarse, and I was damaging the thin walls of the vein even more. So our radio doctor said the stitching should wait until our patient reached a hospital. Meanwhile, we were to continue elevating the foot above the level of his heart, pushing on the wound with a finger, using a pressure bandage for short periods of time, keeping the man warm, injecting penicillin every four hours, and praying. A couple of the patient's relatives and Ron and I took turns keeping vigil at his side during that long night and all next day.

Easter Sunday dawned brilliantly over the Pacific. Was that a sign of hope for us? I wondered. We'd prepared to roast a duck, and we had plans for having some of our co-workers over for dinner. Drums were rolling in the distance—signals for people to move toward the church for the Easter service. Mainao was burning up with fever, and none of us had slept much, but our hearts were brimming with thankfulness that he was still alive.

Drumbeats sounded louder and faster as hundreds of worshipers gathered on the hillside near the church to watch students from the Bible school re-enact the Easter story from the New Testament. Branches from trees and bushes formed small dwellings dotting the area, and as they dramatized the coming of the big earthquake, people inside these "tents" shook the branches while roaring and falling down everywhere. At the same time, someone rolled away a big stone, and a huge "angel" appeared, swathed in a white sheet and complete with white wings. The angel called out: "He is not here. He is alive!" What a wonderful message of hope and life for us on that depressing, frightening day, when we had almost given up hope for this man dying in our house.

We continued to take turns at his side, and meanwhile, we also tried to cook the great duck in the oven of the wood stove. Someone ran down to the vegetable garden and picked green beans, carrots, lettuce, and shallots. Someone peeled potatoes—delicious big potatoes we had bought from our village neighbors. Soon the scrumptious aroma of roasting dinner reached our nostrils, and we realized how hungry we all were.

Yes, Easter dinner was different that year. We had to keep constant vigil, and our celebration did not go exactly as planned, but we were thankful for each hour that Mainao was still alive, and we prayed that he would live until he could get proper help in a hospital. Having our local coworkers join us for dinner gave us support and encouragement during those tense hours, and going ahead with the meal gave all of us a needed diversion as well as the strength and courage to face the hours ahead. However, I didn't think I could ever face cooking duck again. Thus Easter Sunday passed.

Even before dawn on Easter Monday, Ron ran up the steep airstrip to check out the surface. He hurried back to radio the "All clear!" to the pilot, who responded that he would be on the way soon, and that he was bringing a doctor with him—a new man from the United States who needed to see a "bush" station. By then I was so anxious and wound up that I felt like a pressure cooker ready to blow off its lid. We carried our patient up the muddy, narrow footpath to the top of the airstrip, and sat around him, waiting for the hum of the Cessna.

Soon we heard a droning engine. Then we saw the tiny aircraft, appearing out of the blue sky like a small moth. Never before had anything looked so welcome. The plane circled and landed at the bottom of the hill, its little engine revving up to negotiate the steep climb to the top end of the band-aid-sized airstrip. Our pilot stepped out with a curt "Good morning"—after all, this was supposed to be his day off—and out came the doctor. He took a quick look at our patient and said, "He doesn't look too bad. That sore doesn't look like much!" My mouth dropped open, but I dared not utter a word for fear of going into hysterics. We bundled our patient into the plane, the pilot and the doctor got in, we waved, and off they went. Then I burst into tears, with relief and exhaustion as well as considerable anger over the doctor's attitude.

A couple of days later, our regular radio doctor informed us by radio that the youth would not have lived much longer without surgery. He was in extremely bad condition when he arrived at hospital, and he needed emergency surgery plus a hefty blood transfusion immediately. We lost contact with him in subsequent years but were thrilled to hear he was recovering. Once again we were privileged to see a miracle of life.

Fifteen years later, Ron was attending a conference in that district when a man approached and asked if he remembered that young man who had been bleeding so badly. Yes, Ron certainly remembered. The man stuck out his leg and showed a scar. "I was that boy," he said. A very special reunion for these two men followed.

The nightmare of medical work under such frightening conditions brought innumerable blessings. We learned much about life, death, and dying. We developed a tremendous respect for the human body and for the fascinating interrelationships of the body, mind, emotions, and spiritual condition of a human being. Moreover, this way of ministering to our neighbors brought us closer to them than any amount of teaching could possibly have done. We learned to rely on God's promises daily, even hourly.

eight

YOU'VE GOT NO MAIL—YET!

Tapen had two contacts with the outside world: a short-wave radio transceiver and a regular short-wave radio. Living atop our five thousand foot mountain overlooking the vast Pacific Ocean, we sometimes felt the whole world could vanish, or be at war, without our even realizing what was happening. For example, once, when we experienced thirteen unnerving earth tremors all in one dark night, we were fearfully anxious for daylight to come and assure us the world was still there. In other ways we stayed keenly abreast of world events during our months at Tapen. Listening to world news on the radio formed part of our daily ritual, and listening on the two-way radio transceiver at scheduled times became most important for our lives.

This short-wave radio connected us with a base station and neighboring mission stations all over the country at several designated times of each day. This time served not only as community time for isolated mission personnel, but also as a lifeline to medical help whenever we needed advice. Such advice saved lives countless times. Regulations forbade our using the radio just for chitchat, but at certain times we were extremely grateful for the opportunity to share special concerns with the "family" of listeners who, we knew, would pray for us and think of us during a difficult time. The base station decreed that this radio could definitely be used to assure the "physical and spiritual welfare of persons," and we appreciated such opportunities a number of times during our ministry at Tapen.

About once a week, weather permitting, the tiny Cessna aircraft made an early morning trip from the coastal town of Madang to Tapen, a forty-minute flight. Getting ready for this flight often took several hours of the previous day. We had to sort mail, prepare orders, and organize and carefully weigh the airplane's backload of persons, vegetables, or coffee. A capable young church worker at the station arranged for much of this, but the pilot was very particular and insisted that everything be checked again. He was especially concerned that the load would not violate safety standards, since ours was the shortest airstrip in the country; it didn't allow for any leeway for error in taking off and landing on the steep little mountain strip that measured less than eight hundred feet in length.

One month the only plane in the country allowed to land at Tapen was out for extensive maintenance and an overhaul. Our trusty kerosene refrigerator kept our meat fresh until the meat ran out, and after that we managed with some canned meat and local chickens until these, too, ran out. The only store in the area began to run low on supplies, but we and our neighbors had plenty of locally grown fresh fruit and vegetables which we could buy. Our back yard, full of orange and lemon trees, yielded delicious citrus fruit almost year-round, and our vegetable garden produced such succulent goodies as lettuce, tomatoes, rhubarb, green beans, and, occasionally, even a strawberry or two.

Almost daily, neighboring villagers walked over the treacherous mountain trails, carrying bags of potatoes, cabbages, pumpkins, and coffee beans. The coffee beans were for shipping to Madang for sale and export; however, the vegetables were for us to buy, so that the village people could receive some money to purchase kerosene for their lamps as well as precious school supplies for their children.

As the maintenance on our little plane dragged out to three weeks and then four, our supply of diesoline fuel for the power generator ran out, and we resorted to kerosene lanterns for a few hours each evening. Thankfully, our radio battery still produced a strong signal, granting us our daily contact with the outside world.

I searched for a variety of ways to cook cabbage, pumpkins, and potatoes, which formed our staple diet during those weeks. Whenever Ron went on a walking patrol visiting villages, those foods would be his fare for breakfast, lunch, and dinner, so I wasn't keen to serve the same menu each day when he was home. I sought to disguise these three staples so that all three of us would continue to enjoy them. For our almost one-year-old daughter, Joy, a little hand-powered baby food grinder from the USA churned out some interesting combinations of these foods, but she was also old enough to eat most of the same dishes we ate.

Pumpkins fascinated me, and I began to explore interesting ways to cook this vegetable. Some people think pumpkin is only useful for raising hogs and making pies at Thanksgiving and Jack-o-lanterns at Halloween. I boiled and mashed pumpkin, either in the skin or without the skin. We sliced and fried pieces of it, sometimes with the skin, sometimes without. We also cut it open and baked meals in it in our wood fire oven. Sometimes I mashed potatoes and chopped leeks into pumpkin halves, occasionally adding canned corned beef and, rarely, a very expensive delicacy for us called canned tuna. At other times I broke eggs over the "filling" before baking the pumpkin half. Every now and then, when a visitor walked up from the coast, a steep, six-hour climb, he would bring a couple of coconuts. Coconut trees usually didn't grow above an altitude of about three thousand feet, so they were a rare treat from the coast. We could then cook pumpkin pieces in coconut milk, adding a few leaves of cabbage at the last minute, yielding an exotic meal.

Cabbage was not our favorite vegetable, but we learned some interesting ways to fix this, too. When the meat ran out, we found other things to stuff into the cabbage leaves. When steamed cabbage became boring, we stir-fried it with onions and other greens; we also used cabbage in certain casseroles. At other times we fixed a variety of recipes for coleslaw, using home-made dressing.

Chickens didn't thrive very well in that damp, cool climate, but ducks were hardier, and we enjoyed the luxury of cooking and baking with duck eggs. Occasionally, friends from neighboring villages brought a special treat of a huge cassowary egg for us to buy. A cassowary is a large, flightless bird, resembling an ostrich or an emu. The people preferred the egg if the baby cassowary was already well-formed inside, for that way they would be getting more meat. We, however, just could not bring ourselves to eating this kind of egg. If the cassowary egg was fresh, however, I gladly bought it, because one such egg made a very large omelet.

Many times, as we sat around our table feasting on this good food, I thought about stories of Europe and Russia during the war years, when cabbage and potatoes were the only foods available for many refugees. I recalled some Dickens novels which mentioned the same fare, and I realized that such foods contained a lot of nutrition after all. Now, several decades later, we notice how enthusiastically nutritionists promote vegetables such as cabbage as cancer-fighting foods.

Potatoes included several varieties of yams and sweet potatoes, as well as tubers called taro and Chinese taro. These delicious kinds of starchy foods blended in well with the vegetables, and we never really grew tired of them.

Meanwhile, as we continued with our culinary experiments, our radio broadcasts yielded news that the plane was still not available. Our pilot went on vacation, and no other pilot was allowed to fly this particular STOL (Short Take Off and Landing) aircraft. Thus the month extended to five weeks, and then to six.

We yearned for mail much more than we yearned for imported food. There were no phones. We were avid letter writers, and with family members scattered in Papua New Guinea, Australia, the United States, and Germany, mail was our way of keeping the family updated and our way of feeling that we belonged together in spite of the enormous distances separating us. We imagined the letters piling up for us in Madang, and we visualized all kinds of problems happening to family members. I kept imagining how big the mail bag would be, and how we would tip it out and find precious letters. Besides, Joy's birthday was only a couple of days away, and we knew her grandparents would be sending cards.

One evening, at radio time, our pilot announced that he would fly in the next day. We were beside ourselves with excitement, and we hastily added last-minute notes for our families—adding them to the other letters we had written during the previous six weeks.

Next morning dawned, but no airplane came, due to another delay. My disappointment became almost unbearable. But I had enough baking ingredients left to bake a birthday cake, and I thoroughly enjoyed doing that. Checking our vegetable patch a bit later in the day, I found two lonely strawberries so I could even make strawberry frosting for the birthday cake. What more did we need for happiness?

BIRTHDAY DAY dawned, and we fervently hoped it would be MAIL DAY at last. Long before daylight, Ron ran up to the airstrip to check out its surface, then at six o'clock, he had to radio the "All clear" to the pilot, and after that the pilot loaded the plane. I kept nagging my long-suffering husband, "Did you tell him to bring the mail? Are you SURE he'll remember the mail?" I could hardly see straight anymore from all the excitement.

Early that morning, we carried our big dining room table out onto the porch, because later in the day we were planning to have some neighborhood children join us for a little birthday celebration.

Long before the aircraft was due, we trooped up to the top of the airstrip, greeting neighbors, schoolchildren, teachers, and villagers on the way. Everyone joined the single file along our pathway to the airfield. We stood at the top of the hill, gazing into the distance and straining our ears for the high whine of an aircraft. I privately wondered whether, if the pilot had forgotten the mail, I would throw a fit of hysteria, like people were accustomed to doing in the old novels. We stood staring at the low gap between the towering mountains, breathing in the fresh mountain air and whispering between silent pauses for listening.

Slowly, wisps of clouds began to appear on distant mountains, and I almost panicked. *What if the clouds sock us in before the plane arrives? What if he can't land? What if all that mail will have to go back again to Madang?* I looked around at the other people and noticed their expressions of somewhat detached anticipation. They really didn't seem very concerned at all. After all, they had managed for hundreds of years without ever having an airplane or any mail come. They probably thought we white people were a bit obsessed about this mail business.

More clouds joined the first wisps, and soon a thick bank of clouds became visible. The clouds, like white sails of ancient galleons, formed strikingly beautiful patterns against the infinite blue of the sky.

Someone said, "Listen." Sure enough, we heard a distant whine of an engine. A few seconds later someone pointed to a black speck in the sky. It grew and grew. Our pilot deftly maneuvered the little plane between the clouds, through the gap, and circled the airstrip. The airplane vanished again for a minute while preparing for its final approach. It came closer and closer. *Please don't let it crash now, Lord!* Suddenly it roared onto the bottom end of the airstrip, touched ground, and revved up the engines to roll up to the top of the strip. Finally, the bird had landed.

As soon as the propeller was silent, our pilot opened the window, then the door, and climbed out. Soon we unloaded the plane and the pod. Out came two enormous mail bags. I feasted my eyes on those bags, almost transfixed. Out came some meat and other supplies, as well as some urgently-needed medicines. We visited for a few minutes with the pilot, and helped him load the plane again for his return to Madang.

In a procession we filed back down the side of the airstrip toward our house, lugging bags and other goods. Our dining room table, sitting out of its usual place on the porch, became a perfect locale for the ritual of tipping out the mail. We heaved the two heavy bags up onto the table, and together we poured out its content. I immediately wanted to grab our personal letters and vanish somewhere to read them, but Ron said we should help together to sort the mail for everyone. *How can he be so unconcerned when I am dying for news? Have I not waited long enough for this moment?* Grudgingly, I leaned over the table and helped Ron sort the mail. After all, this mail was for the whole area, and others had just as much right to their letters as we did to ours.

Joy sensed the excitement of the morning. She knew it was a special day, but, at one, she didn't really understand what a birthday was all about. She excitedly strained at my leg to get up and be part of the action. We lifted her up to show her the mail. We decided to get the camera and take a picture. She wanted to help sort, so we deposited her in the middle of that broad, capacious table, and she promptly began to help us sort, reaching out for envelopes, clapping her hands together with glee, throwing periodicals and letters in all directions, but, mercifully, refraining from eating any of the stuff. She realized that today the table was not covered with food. Her enthusiasm soon infected us all with joy, and we chatted and giggled as we sorted mail.

At last, the mountain of mail gave way to neat piles of letters, magazines, packages of books, and other mail, and people began to carry away their piles. The Schardts' pile was left, and we decided that to make sense of our letters, we'd better sort them first according to the dates stamped on the envelopes, in order to get our families' news in some sort of chronological order. By this time we needed to sit, so we dragged chairs to the table and sat down, arranging the mail in various little piles.

Finally, we tore open the first letter from our folks, and tears of relief and thankfulness filled my eyes as I began to read. At last the long wait was over. Soon we cleared the table of mail and brought out the goodies for Joy's birthday party. As other toddlers arrived with their mothers, we began a very special celebration.

nine

FEEDING THE EIGHTY

Flying from the city of Lae into Boana in a single-engine Cessna plane was a spectacular experience. The airplane took off from the Lae runway, which ended at the Lae harbor. In the nineteen sixties, we took off right over a wrecked ship which had been there since World War Two and was always sinking a bit further into the harbor floor. By 1971, only a tip of the prow was still visible above water, but we had a great view of it as we took off from Lae. Twelve minutes of flying over the trees while steadily gaining altitude brought us to the crest of the Rawlingson Ranges, which fringed the big Markham River Valley. The pilot steered over the crest and began a wide ring inside mountains encircling Boana, our home from 1966 through 1970.

Boana served as a mission station, government patrol post, village, and agricultural station on a mountain ringed by steep river gorges. We had the impression of traveling to a castle surrounded by a deep moat, except that there wasn't a draw bridge. Villages and hamlets dotted the mountainsides in all directions, resembling minute brown specks in the lush green jungle carpet. Lazy wisps of smoke curled their way up from some of the tiny brown specks. On many days large powder puffs of cumulus clouds hugged the mountain tops like whipped topping on inverted blue ice cream cones, and sometimes the pilot had a hard time finding a hole through which he could fly into our area. On such days, he gained altitude by spiraling ever higher right above our station until he could look down and see a hole. He'd then swoop down like a bird of prey, have a quick look over the airfield to make sure no kids or cows were on it, and in a very short time, he would land.

Meanwhile, people came running from all directions, converging onto the grassy airfield. Our coffee agent had to get his bags of coffee ready to ship out; the patrol officer had papers and mail to send; the medical aid post orderly had a seriously ill patient to send to hospital; gardeners wanted to send baskets of fresh vegetables to sell in town; the missionary and congregation had mail and an evangelist family to send to a new area; and young and old alike were curious to see who was coming and who was going. Everyone stood in awe of the pilot, wondering what magical powers he must possess to be able to get that heavy vehicle to go up in the air and fly as though it were a light bird.

During part of our time in Boana, only fifteen minutes' flight away, we had the wonderful privilege of having my parents, Frieda and Martin, live and work in Lae. My father died in 1968, but Mother continued to work there until 1981, when she retired to Australia. In 1969, our joy knew no bounds when Ron's parents, Martha and Arthur, arrived from the USA to serve as volunteer missionaries for about a year—first they were house-parents in the Central Highlands area of the country and then they served a congregation in Lae. How we treasured the rare times when they could take off for a few days and fly in on the little Cessna aircraft to be part of our lives in Boana. They enjoyed helping with our community activities and also with a big new church-building project. Thus, when we needed to travel to Lae for medical care and meetings, we relished visits with three grandparents!

Walking in the Boana area presented a drama of its own quite apart from flying; besides, it required a lot of stamina. Most of the villages of our circuit dotted the mountainsides on the other side of the "moat;" in order to get to any of those villages, one had to clamber down steep muddy paths which zigzagged for a thousand feet downwards to the slippery, rocky banks of a treacherously swift torrent called the Bonzok River. Village children usually guided us to crossing places which they called bridges, but which I called death traps. At one place several logs were thrown across the gorge, and I remember inching my way across these rotting logs, listening to the roar of the current beneath us as it crashed against the huge boulders millions of years old. When my courage failed me, I gratefully accepted the arm of a local guide, who cheered me up during the crossing by citing the names of various acquaintances of his who had fallen in and perished "over there by that rock."

Occasionally, a bridge actually had a side for crossers to hang on, but invariably, the actual bridge was woven from jungle vines in such a way that there were huge gaps across which one had to step gingerly to avoid a flying leap into the frothy waters below. Hanging on to a side which consisted of a single strand of jungle twine swaying out above the bridge did not provide much of a sense of security, even though this handrail was anchored to various tree branches by means of other vines. The unspoken engineering motto seemed to indicate that if the bridge was made of logs, no side was needed; if, on the other hand, the bridge was woven from vines, a vine handrail was necessary.

Once we completed the crossing, we began the zigzag on the other side again, ever ascending until we had to cross over into another valley. In four or five hours of walking in this mountain range, we often had to cross several more streams, and sometimes we did not have the benefit of bridges like those over the Bonzok. Walking through a stream was almost worse than crossing a bridge; however, thanks to the help of the strong, brown hands of our patient travel companions, we made it across safely. Because the stream beds were often rough, full of sharp slippery stones, we sometimes had to keep our shoes on for crossing. Once I lost one walking shoe while crossing a stream, but that hobble home might need to be narrated another time.

We ourselves did not make nearly as many trips over these kinds of trails as the village people made, and I often admired their cheerfulness and good nature, when they had to spend so much of their time on dangerous trails, crossing wild rivers and carrying heavy bags of coffee, food, store supplies, or sick children.

The people spent much time walking on these rugged paths, not only for carrying supplies and children, but also for attending church and church meetings, participating in courses and retreats, and tending to government and clan matters. Often, the men of the congregations had more opportunities to take part in courses and retreats than women had. Such events included in-service for pastors or teachers, training seminars for evangelists, and meetings at the patrol post for village councilors. The women, however, despite their very active participation and leadership in congregational life in the villages, often had to stay home. For this reason, we planned to have a course just for women.

We carefully wrote out invitations to all the village congregations to send a representative or two, and together with our church colleagues, we eagerly planned our Bible studies, teaching strategies, teaching aids, and meals. We wondered whether anyone would come. We could handle up to thirty women quite well, we thought, and I ordered some hamburger meat to be flown in from Lae to supplement the diet of sweet potatoes, taro, rice, and greens which we planned.

By the end of arrival day, eighty women had appeared. They came from all over the mountainous circuit; some had to walk for two days to get to Boana. They were all really excited about having a course just for them. We were floored, wondering how we would ever be able to feed all those people. We feared we'd run out of firewood and food; besides, we needed more floor space for sleeping. Everyone rallied and rose to the occasion. Our neighbors and local village people went to their gardens to dig up more sweet potatoes. We found a classroom with a thatched roof and clean earthen floor on which some of the overflow could sleep. I found some vegetables in our little garden and started chopping them up to make the meat pot go further.

Under the huge sprawling shade umbrella of a casuarina tree, some men came and hammered smooth wooden poles into the ground. Then they used long narrow poles to form a frame for a table-top, and on it some of the women wove bamboo strips. An elegant long table began to take shape. Soon long green banana leaves covered the woven table top, and the table stood ready for the feast.

I had three puny pounds of hamburger meat ready to cook for this first evening meal. How would we ever feed all those women with this tiny amount of meat? At the same time I was really thankful for the big group that came, and we prayed that there would somehow be enough for all to enjoy the course. I carefully chopped several leeks from the garden and added some celery stalks and spinach leaves. We scraped some carrots and chopped them. After thoroughly browning the meat on our wood stove, I transferred it to a large pot and added lots of water and the chopped vegetables, iodized salt, and a few spices. The pot simmered along, and soon it was ready. Meanwhile, some of the other women peeled and cooked the sweet potatoes, and we cooked a big pot of rice over an open fire. We carried all our pots of food over to the shady patch under a large casuarina tree.

The women in the thatched roof kitchen stood around in a circle and sang a prayer in their language. Then every visitor lined up to receive the food which we had prepared. The women kept coming and coming. Some had babies along, and others had toddlers with them. Each one reached out her plate, and we filled it. When all were served, they sat around under the shady trees and ate. We were amazed to see that enough food remained to satisfy all of us cooks, too. It wasn't only a feast. It was a miracle!

Fitting all those women into the little classroom would have to be another miracle. Somehow, however, we managed, and the course began smoothly. We joined their enthusiastic voices in praise and prayer. They sang beautiful melodies right from their hearts in the Kotte language, and as I joined them, as always, the songs brought happy tears to my eyes.

The next three days were incredibly busy as we taught, sang, cooked, ate, and studied together. Babies toddled in and out as their mothers strained to hear the Bible stories; they marveled at the narration and unfolding of God's plan for all people. Chalkboard diagrams, posters, dramatizations, and pictures all enhanced the story. Many of the women had had minimal schooling, but their faith was alive, thanks to the Spirit and caring teachers and evangelists. They could jump up at short notice and dramatize a Bible story, and they were willing to share experiences from their home villages. They shared struggles and joys about witnessing for Jesus. In addition, the miracle of food continued, and each day we found enough to satisfy everyone.

Women's conference at Boana

ten

SEASIDE SERVINGS

For many veterans of the Second World War, the word "Finschhafen" conjures up nightmarish memories of endless rains, muddy jungle trails, and enemy attacks, as well as debilitating attacks of malaria. Decisive battles for the recapture of New Guinea from Japanese forces took place in the Finschhafen area, and during certain weeks, thousands of infantrymen from the Allied troops were stationed there. Bombing was severe—first by Japanese troops and later by the Allies. Heavy bombing attacks devastated vital food gardens, destroyed homes, killed people, and left huge, gaping holes throughout the land. As the months went by, the tropical rains brought life back to the land, and many of these bomb craters became covered with grass.

Finschhafen had been part of my own family history for many years, and now, in 1971, after serving in the Boana area for several years, we were assigned to mission work at Heldsbach in the Finshhafen area. Heldsbach became our home for the next eleven years, and during those years, our daughters Joy and Heidi were joined by two more siblings, Natalie and Graham. Some of our happiest family memories of those years centered at Nugidu Beach.

Nugidu, seven miles from our house, snuggled leeward on a peninsula sheltering Finschhafen's Maneba Harbor. The peninsula's tip had a coral-bed airstrip built for small aircraft, and whenever we landed on this strip on the tiny peninsula flanked by shimmering coral reefs visible under the brilliant aquamarine ocean, we felt like we were landing on an aircraft carrier. Nothing quite matched the sensation of circling over Nugidu airstrip, banking for final approach, and flying in to alight on the tip of this finger in the blue Pacific.

Nugidu beach served as a marvelous haven and stress reliever for our family during our busy years in Finschhafen. With thirteen years spanning the births of our eldest and youngest children, and with no television, no movie theaters, and no restaurants around, we found the beach a wonderful getaway for all age groups. Here we renewed ourselves, exercised, and relaxed physically, psychologically, and spiritually. Yes, Nugidu served as a matchless retreat. During those years, we had many visitors, both locally and from overseas, and a trip to Nugidu became a popular outing whenever company came. Sitting on the warm sand, overlooking the harbor and the distant hills westwards, and watching the ever-changing hues of tropical sunsets, we shared precious insights, problems, and joys.

Arriving at the beach, everyone tumbled out of the car, grabbed towels, food, and drinks, and charged down to the water's edge. We sank into the warm water, took deep breaths, and swam out into the deep. Some donned snorkeling gear and decided to check out the rainbow-colored fish along the reef out by the harbor's entrance; others floated or rolled over and over in the sea; sometimes we gathered in a circle in the deep water, chatting while treading water and getting in a bit of aerobics that way. At other times we lay on the sand, watching the view while chuckling over crabs scurrying sideways over our legs.

Years before, an old tree on the beach had broken loose after suffering decades of pounding waves and had fallen across the beach, its highest branches reaching across the water. By now its leaves had long vanished, and years of sun and saltwater had left its trunk and limbs glistening white and smooth, serving as a perfect jumping and diving board for the children. About twenty yards from shore, a big brown rock filled with delightful and fascinating crevices lay firm and immovable just beneath the ever-undulating seawater, attracting hundreds of brilliantly colorful fish, which would dart in and out of the holes. Those of us who disliked deep-sea diving gained much fascination from watching the fish in the clear aquamarine brine.

As our children's swimming skills became stronger, they ventured farther and farther from shore, causing their parents some anxiety. After we sighted a shark and some other rather large fish there, however, the children contented themselves with staying a little closer to the beach while swimming.

Frequently, a little coastal boat came into view, entering the harbor and gliding in to the dock, which was just out of sight beyond a bend in the harbor channel. The boat plowed through the sea, frothing at the prow, making huge waves which reached us where we were swimming and sent us rocking. We threw up our hands and waved gleefully at passengers dotting the side of the ship, and often we heard the murmur of their voices over the lapping waves.

At the call of "Time to eat," happily squealing bodies leaped out of the shimmering ocean, and people clambered up, dripping and shaking off water while racing one another to the "table."

Our dining table at this beach was a sheet covering a lumpy stretch of salty sand, battened down by plates and thermos jugs at the corners. The cloth often held home-baked rolls, a big plastic canister filled with cold spaghetti salad, including, among other ingredients, canned tuna or cooked chicken cubes, freshly chopped tomatoes, cucumbers, canned cheese cubes, and chives, tossed together with home-made salad dressing and fresh lime juice. At one corner of this table sat a wooden bowl filled with big chunks of succulent tropical fruits such as bananas, pineapple, and papaya. Sometimes we built a fire on the sand to roast corn ears and sweet potatoes. The children enjoyed getting their fingers messy and relaxing their eating manners somewhat, and so did Dad and Mom. After all, the water was just inches away, and we could drop in and wash off greasy fingers quite easily.

Getting ready to eat, we positioned ourselves in such a way that we all had a good view of the waves lapping at the beach's edge. Beyond the waves, we watched the hills on the other side of the usually calm harbor. As the sun was about to set, it offered a festival of color changes while gilding the clouds which hugged the mountain tops. Munching at our food, we kept pointing to new cloud formations, outguessing one another about what the clouds looked like at that moment. Sometimes we saw God's "face," and sometimes we saw different animal shapes. Inevitably, these sights led to questions and deeper discussions about life, death, and infinity. I recalled my father's favorite psalm, while I lifted my eyes to the hills and drank in this gift of beauty from God—the God who brought help and who neither slumbered nor slept (Psalm 121).

A light splash in the distance often interrupted our musings, and we lowered our eyes from the heavens to see Spanish mackerel leaping out of the sea, high up into the air, and back down again. What entertainment!

All of a sudden, the sun vanished. In the tropics, once the sun set behind the mountains, darkness fell in a hurry, so we had to quickly gather our things while we could still see. We began slapping our arms as mosquitoes buzzed our camp; clearly, it was time to return home. As we piled into the car for our bumpy ride home over the old coral road (constructed during the Second World War by Allied troops), we sang all the way home. We were ready for work again.

Now we live hundreds of miles from the nearest ocean beach, and Nugidu is a dream getaway from our past. But we realize we still need a "Nugidu," a place where we can lay aside the burdens of life for an hour or two, a place which reminds us of God's magnificent creation. A shady tree sometimes provides such a respite, or a visit to a nearby park. During winter, a flowering pot plant near the glass doors, with a sugar-like backdrop of snow on the deck outside, provides a "Nugidu." Even taking time to watch birds for a few minutes sends my spirit soaring.

Perhaps each of us needs a place which we can recognize as a haven from the stresses of everyday life. Not that we need to shut out our everyday concerns at such a place; on the contrary, as we relax and contemplate, and as we dare to share some of these concerns with family or caring friends, we gain new insights about them. We also may just contemplate life's mysteries in silence as we drink in the views.

eleven

WIDEN THE CIRCLE

Every three weeks, a ship called the *MV Simbang* plied our coastline, calling in at ports along the ragged shore, delivering people and goods, picking up seriously ill persons for the hospital, and loading coffee for export and market goods for the big markets in the town of Lae. A *Simbang* trip was a big social occasion: villagers burdened with bags of coconuts, coffee beans, and personal goods walked for many hours, streaming from all directions toward the harbor. As they gathered near the jetty, they cleared small patches of ground, swung down their heavy loads, and sat down cross-legged in small, chattering clusters. Soon one person collected a few dry twigs and piled them into the center of a cluster, while others searched in their pockets for a damp matchbox, struck a match, and coaxed a reluctant little wisp of smoke into flames. Not that the weather was cold; on the contrary, the temperature was mostly in the upper eighties, with the humidity right up there with the temperature. A fire, however, symbolized community and sharing.

During our years in Finschhhafen, the *MV Simbang* became a vital part of our lives, and we eagerly scanned the horizon for signs of its arrival on those scheduled days.

Passage down the northeast coast from the port of Madang to Finschhafen sometimes included rough seas, so we never knew how long the journey would take. At times, the ship was delayed, because loading took longer at the previous port of call, or because it had to wait for a patient who urgently needed to get to a hospital. In such a case, a runner would go ahead and notify the captain to delay departure while relatives hurried as quickly as possible, carrying the patient to the ship.

In Papua New Guinea, many of life's most important transactions took place around a fire. People sat in a circle, forming an instant community. Around a fire they passed betel nuts to one another, followed by a container of lime. Around the fire they passed a refreshing green coconut into which they'd punched a hole, and everyone in the circle took a deep draft of the magnificently refreshing coconut juice. Around the fire lively discussions took place—discussions about life, death, faith, money, evil spirits, and the Good Spirit. Around the fire, especially after nightfall, people dared to reveal dark secrets, personal fears, and agonizing problems. Around the fire they vigorously grappled with ethical decisions, planned betrothals, arranged marriages, and negotiated bride gift exchanges. Around the fire the Christians held their Bibles, dog-eared and worn, and they leaned in toward the light of the flame, searching for the verses which helped provide guidance for their vital decisions.

Whenever we went to the wharf, we saw such circles of people decking the ground along the water's edge and on either side of the road. A person seldom sat alone anywhere. Someone arriving or standing alone would inevitably receive a wave from someone else to join a group. Sometimes the new person was a complete stranger; at other times this person was a distant acquaintance or relative of someone in the group.

When we'd arrive at the wharf and join the waiting crowd, we would hear a hum of murmurs from groups of women, men, and children huddled around the fires. Every now and then, laughter exploded from a group, and other groups chuckled along with the happy ones, even if they didn't hear the joke. Who says laughter isn't contagious?

Soon the boat slid into view, its engines purring at low revs, and we all rose from the ground and meandered toward the narrow wooden wharf, straining to recognize someone among the people in the crowd leaning over the ship's upper deck rails. The gentle swish of the boat cutting through the serene water in the harbor blended with little shouts of recognition as persons on shore waved to loved ones on board.

Within a few minutes, the ship began to reverse in order to slow down even more, and gently it glided toward the pier. As crew members threw the bow and stern ropes ashore, strong hands on the wharf grasped the ropes and looped them over sturdy iron holders. A minute later, at the command of the captain in the wheelhouse, the ship's engines spluttered and died, and soon a crude metal gangplank bridged the ship and the wharf. Passengers crowded toward the wharf, balancing their heavy bags by leaning forward almost double; others passed their bags down to waiting relatives and friends on shore beneath them. Once again, the *MV Simbang* had docked.

Finschhafen's harbor received splendid protection by way of the long isthmus called Nugidu jutting out into the Pacific. This harbor achieved fame during World War Two, for much naval activity took place from this setting. Heavy bombing by the Allies during the recapture of this land from enemy occupation resulted in a profusion of heavy metal littered throughout the magnificent harbor area, both inside the water and in the lush green jungle surrounding it. At the end of the war, the Allies dumped thousands of barrels and other no-longer-needed equipment into the harbor to settle among bombed ships on the harbor floor. A few years later, an enterprising young entrepreneur from Australia made a fortune hauling these barrels out of the water and selling them as scrap iron to Japan.

Our mission house sat on a coral hill about two hundred and forty feet above sea level, overlooking the ocean. Since we lived seven miles north of the harbor, we usually saw the ship approaching about an hour before it actually docked at the wharf. That gave us plenty of time to gather passengers and cargo and head down to the wharf in the station truck or land-rover.

One sultry week in January, the hottest month of the year, the *Simbang* was due around five o'clock in the afternoon. January was summer vacation month for that part of the world. Finschhafen had summer all year long, so we never spoke about summer vacation, just about holidays.

This week it was Ron's turn to make the trip to the ship, so when we sighted the boat we passed the word around the station, and people gathered near the truck with their goods and their relatives. I casually mentioned to Ron as he left, that in case someone needed to get off the boat to stretch for a few hours, he could bring the traveler up to the house for supper. The truck then left.

An hour later I went into the kitchen to prepare a bit of dinner when I heard the truck coming back up the hill. I looked out and noticed that it was full of people. Wondering why Ron wasn't dropping them off at their destinations, I noticed that he drove right up to our house and stopped. People began piling out. Ron walked over to me and said, "Well, Dearie, I found a number of people who needed a few hours off the boat. The ship won't leave until ten o'clock tonight, and these people want to see the area."

"Yes, but who is going to feed them," I whispered fiercely.

"I guess we are," came his smiling reply.

My mind was racing. What did I have in the kitchen to feed twenty-one strangers? The nearest grocery store was seven hours' boat trip away! Darkness was setting in. Our neighbors and villagers who faithfully brought supplies of fruit and vegetables for us to buy had gone home.

"Sure, let them come in," I said carelessly, and I walked outside to greet them all. There were two large families and several single people and a couple of children as well. Many of them came from the highlands, where they were working as missionaries and agriculturists. People streamed into our house and made themselves comfortable. They were all friendly and they looked like an interesting assortment of personalities.

Meanwhile, I surveyed the kitchen. I noted there was not enough bread left to go around. There sat a huge golden pumpkin begging to be scrubbed and baked, while a pile of sweet potatoes lay on the counter. The freezer compartment of our kerosene refrigerator yielded a big plastic bag full of juicy fillets of some mackerel, which Ron had caught recently while fishing. In the vegetable basket lay a plump head of cabbage flanked by a few scrawny shallots and several firm, green cucumbers. While our unexpected guests, chatting happily, admired orchids in the yard and took turns visiting our one and only rest room, Ron and I soaked the frozen mackerel in water to thaw it out—this was before the age of the microwave, after all—and we grabbed a knife and a peeler and set to work on the vegetables. Soon one rack in the gas oven held a huge cookie tray packed with bright orange wedges of pumpkin; I'd topped each piece with a bit of salt and margarine. In the rack below lay several rows of scrubbed sweet potatoes. After a while, the big cast iron roasting dish served as a frying pan for me to fry big white chunks of mackerel, rolled in seasoned flour. In a big saucepan next to the mackerel, the sliced cabbage steamed away for a few minutes. Peeling and slicing the cucumbers, I added some chopped shallots and tossed this salad with my home-made mayonnaise.

Twenty-one of us sat in a capacious circle in the dining-living room, and after singing grace, we filed around the round table to get our food. We had a feast. To my surprise, everyone received a big plate full of food, and our lively discussion continued right until it was time to take this friendly crowd back to the ship. Two hours earlier we hadn't known one another at all. Now we were new friends.

In ensuing years we often met one or another of these persons, when on leave, or at a conference or retreat, and we realized that the special bond created that night, over a hastily-prepared meal, despite my initial un-generous attitude, nevertheless provided new blessings.

Years later, a young woman in her twenties came with a singing group from the USA to sing and share her faith in various areas in Papua New Guinea. We discovered to our surprise that she had been one of the children at our home that night.

Countless times we widened the circle for unexpected guests around the table. If they didn't fit around the table, we widened the circle to the room's edge or onto the porch. Somehow, the food stretched, and inevitably, we experienced a new understanding of grace and friendship.

twelve

ROCKING TABLE

One night an urgent message came from Lae, calling me to be with my mother who was in hospital there. Although Lae was only about a hundred miles from Finschhafen, no vehicle road joined the two places, so we had to travel either by ship or by airplane to get there.

Weather predictions made flying an uncertain option that week. I checked the boat schedule and discovered a boat was scheduled to come through Finschhafen later that evening, on its way to Lae. We decided I would take our baby daughter along to the ship and check for space for us to go along. Since this was school vacation time, many students would be traveling, and the boat might already be booked out.

I hastily threw together some clothes and diapers, grabbed a cardboard box, and lined it with some towels. That was to be Natalie's bunk-bed on board, in case we'd be up on the windy deck. A few hours later, we climbed into the truck and joined other hopeful passengers who wanted to go to Lae.

The wharf undulated with crowds of people clamoring to obtain tickets and get on board the ship. I joined the line and eventually made it to the window. The clerk advised that there was one free bunk, so I purchased a ticket. Soon willing hands were helping to lift my daughter and propel me up the gangway into the ship.

People kept piling onto the boat, and crew members were checking tickets as carefully as possible. Soon the engines of the boat began to roar into action, and within a few minutes a crew member loosened the cables and, as the engines sprang into reverse, the boat eased away from the wharf, plowing through the black water on this dark night. Amid much waving and shouting across the water between wharf and boat, we glided out toward the harbor, the captain skillfully avoiding shallow waters near a tiny island in the middle of the harbor, skirting a reef at the mouth of the bay, and heading the ship out into the choppy open sea.

I settled Natalie onto the bunk, but that miniscule cabin became insufferably hot and stuffy, since the ventilation system wasn't working. Presently I tried to lie down, too, for I felt somewhat unsteady on my legs. The sea became rougher, and our tiny porthole kept lighting up with flashes of lightning. Sure enough, a storm was brewing at sea. Our ship bobbed up and down, plowing through the rough waves and throwing up masses of saltwater over the bow with each wave.

Our cabin adjoined the small dining area of the boat, and around the two dining tables sat people who did not have anywhere to sleep. I heard some commotion and moaning coming from that area, and I got up to investigate the problem. One student was sitting among the others with his head in his hands, moaning. When I asked him what was wrong, he complained of terrible pain in the head. His eyes were wild-looking, and he wasn't really making much sense when he was speaking, even though I could speak and understand his language. I was afraid that he was delirious. With no way to obtain medical help on board that crowded boat, it seemed important to get him to lie flat. I knew he should go onto a bunk, and I had one of the only indoor bunks. Having him sleep on one of the drafty double bunks upstairs on the deck would be cruel and dangerous, but I was a bit resentful about having to give up our bed. However, within a couple of minutes, Dembeng was lying on my bunk, and Natalie was lying in the middle of the dining room table, while I sat in the tiny spot vacated by our patient. A passenger obtained a wet cloth to help keep him cool in the stuffy cabin, and soon his moaning eased somewhat.

Meanwhile, I took a look around me and, propping up my tired head, I struck up a conversation with the total strangers sitting around the table with me on this eeriest of midnights. The trip would last at least five more hours, so we decided we might as well get acquainted. There wasn't much chance we could catch some sleep, although the babies lying at assorted angles on the tabletop were sleeping, albeit somewhat fitfully. Not even the proverbial sardine would have had room to squeeze in, but we were safe so far, and no one was seasick yet, so those were two positives for us on the crowded vessel. Later, when a crew member stuck his head down into the dining room, I dared to ask him whether the boat had enough life jackets on board, and he assured me that it did. This relieved me enormously, even though I had no idea if he actually knew the answer to my question. Also, I had no idea how I would hang on to a baby and a life jacket, should an emergency arise. Next time a friendly crew man poked his head down below deck, I cheerfully asked him if he knew how many passengers were on board. Smiling, he replied, "Plenty," and all of us chorused in cheerful agreement.

Around two in the morning, the lightning flashed every few seconds, and soon we heard crashes of thunder above the roar of the engines. I tried to recall what I'd read about incidents when lightning had struck the masts of ships, and the recollection brought no comfort. I looked around, and only then it came to me that Natalie and I were the only white persons on board this very crowded ship. That didn't scare me a bit, for all the people were caring and solicitous, willing to help us, but I couldn't help wondering how some people would feel in that position. There'd been many times the past years when any other white person had been at least 40 minutes' flight or two days' walk away, and for us this had been a completely natural circumstance.

Sitting propped up during the wee hours of that morning around a ship's dining table, packed in among lots of heavily breathing, similarly propped up persons all trying to help the long night to pass more quickly, I had a lot of opportunity to observe my traveling companions. Their beautiful brown faces told many stories. Wonderfully infectious laughter frequently punctuated their animated conversations, as one after the other thought of an anecdote or story to share. Many of them spoke in a language which I understood, while others came from different language areas of Papua New Guinea. However, even when they told stories, we all joined in with the laughter anyway, because we had become a closely knit community in those few hours.

I asked my cozy companions whether we were in danger from the storm, and they shrugged and replied that we probably weren't. But I could tell that a couple of the women were afraid like I was. So we shared knowing, anxious glances when we thought the others weren't watching us. Every now and then we checked up on the student, who was getting worse by the minute. What a helpless feeling we had. I prayed that he would survive the trip and that we could get him to the hospital as soon as the ship berthed. Lightning pierced the whole area, and thunder roared deafeningly even above the engine's rattle. Our ship, bucking in all directions at times, moved on through the waters.

Presently I noticed that we were way out to sea, and I was afraid the captain had lost his bearings. Someone quickly assured me that on a night like this it was safer far away from land and from potential reefs. I decided we were too far out for me to worry about how I would clamber ashore in shallow water in case of shipwreck.

Minutes passed. Hours passed. There we sat around a table that now served as a multi-bed for babies, while a rim of sturdy, loving arms encircled it. To be sure, this table lacked food, drinks, silverware, and plates; however, it reverberated with authentic and unforgettable table fellowship. Soon a couple of toddlers who had been snoozing in their mothers' arms awakened from our babble, stirred, stretched, and clamored for some food. We reached into our *bilums* (string bags), and found snacks. One woman had an ear of cold corn, which she'd roasted in ashes before the journey. Another brought out a baked sweet potato, which she'd carefully wrapped in a small cloth. Yet another unwrapped a *wopa biskit,* a salty hard cracker resembling a teething rusk—a favorite quick breakfast food for people on bush patrol. I had a few crackers and a bit of fruit along. One of the men broke out a bunch of betel nut, found his small round can of powdered calcium, and offered this snack. Suddenly we all realized we were hungry. We shared whatever we had and nibbled together. No one needed baby bottles and formula. Those of us with babies were nursing mothers, and when our babies required a drink, they received nourishment, sterile and at a perfect temperature, straight from Mom, even on this wild and scary night. And so we nibbled and chatted away as we bumped arms which formed a continuous wall around the table.

Pounding rain soon joined the relentless clamor of engines and the intermittent explosions of thunder, and within seconds it was pouring down, streaming through the ship in rivulets, mixed with the foaming seawater, which continued to crash over the front of the ship. The rain was a relief for us, for we gained the distinct impression that the sea was beginning to calm a little as soon as the heavy rain started.

Dawn appeared at last—first a light grey inkblot on the black horizon, and then, when the rain eased, a smattering of pale apricot rouge which turned into a fiery crimson ball rising out of the ocean. We all sighed, shifted, and stared at one another with glazed looks. Our faces were grey and puffy around our sunken eyes from lack of sleep, but our spirits soared as we craned our necks to see through the portholes and began to make out the ragged coastline, while the rocking ship continued to churn its way through foamy waves toward Lae.

Happy human sounds wafted over us from the deck above, and even the thunderclaps finally, finally quieted down, with intervals between lightning and thunder mercifully lengthening. Our thoughts turned to our plans for disembarking and for getting to our destinations once we were ashore. Our patient stirred and groaned frequently, and a couple of us extricated ourselves from our positions and, teetering and banging our way on the rolling floor to his cabin, we checked him. He was delirious, mumbling incoherently in a strange tongue. *Dear God, please let him live until we can get help for him,* I breathed. Reeling with nausea, I tottered back to my place at table and sat down again, resting my head on my arms.

Suddenly the ship stopped rocking, the noisy clatter of the engine softened, and we stared at one another in questioning alarm. *What was that? Engine trouble? Are we sinking?* We looked out. We were entering calm waters of the harbor, and we were almost there. Noisy giggles of relief and thankfulness filled the dank little galley, and we scrambled up out of our places, stretched, shook ourselves, and gathered up our bundles of babies and clothing.

As our boat approached the wharf, the rain began again. This was a frequent gesture of welcome from Lae, where the annual rainfall measured over two hundred inches. We staggered up the steep narrow stairs to the deck above and joined dozens of other passengers who were leaning over the rails, straining to watch our ship berth and to detect some acquaintances among the crowds waiting at shore. Our captain cut the engines, and our boat glided toward the wharf. But the wharf was packed with boats of various sizes and shapes, berthed two deep out from the dock. There was no room for us. We watched as the boat inched its way closer to the other boats, and soon our boat came to rest alongside another boat. We looked at one another in disbelief. Yes, we had arrived, but we were two boats' width away from land. Crew members announced that we would have to cross the other two boats and disembark that way.

We called out for a stretcher or cot for Dembeng, and we asked one of the nimble young men who would alight first, if he'd arrange with the harbor crew that someone go and try to call the hospital for an ambulance. We gathered our babies and goods and lined up awkwardly to negotiate this crazy crossing in pouring rain. We became a continuous human line of stumbling legs and helping hands as we negotiated the first jump over our own ship's side into the next ship, then across that loaded deck over the opposite side and into the second boat, across that boat and over that side onto a very wobbly, steeply angled gangplank with no railing, and finally onto the wharf. Our babies went from one pair of arms to the next; our bags followed, and after each successful crossing we stopped, dropped our things, turned around, and gave a hand to the person following.

Thus our unique table fellowship circle broke up. Each of us had a mission here in Lae; each of us had to go a different direction. We had shared an unforgettable night. We thanked one another and said farewell. We waited at the wharf until a vehicle came to pick up our patient for hospital. I hastily scribbled a note to send along for the doctor, describing his symptoms along the journey, saying I would check with the hospital very soon. At last, holding Natalie, I could climb into a van which took us, along with many others, to the guest house, where we could shower and change before going to the hospital to visit the patients. My mother was indeed very ill, but within a few days she recovered. Dembeng, it was established, had suffered a mild stroke—and this really puzzled the medical staff, since he was only about nineteen years old. He could speak four languages, but when he was struck ill, he could only speak his mother tongue and could not speak any of the other languages. Thankfully, he made a good recovery, even though it was slow. Within weeks he was able to speak his other languages again, and he returned to school in Finschhafen to complete his training as an agricultural teacher.

thirteen

WATERFALL

Waterfalls remind us of the wonders of nature as well as the amazing power of rivers. Often, a river begins with a small spring or brook at its source and grows as it winds for many miles among hills and along valleys, forever yearning to empty into another river or into the great ocean. What a miracle that rivers, if not polluted, cleanse themselves in an incredibly short distance. Countless peoples from many cultures have harnessed the power of water in many creative ways, while countless others have killed the life of rivers through pollution. We can't help asking ourselves where we stand as a nation today in our relationship with rivers—the waters for our earth's life.

While we lived in Papua New Guinea, our family's favorite swimming spot was a deep hole in the Butaweng River. Walking upriver, we found numerous waterfalls cascading over smooth gray rocks. Stately forest trees and long tendrils of lianas mingled with majestic fern plants to form spectacular frames for every view of the river, but the best view was right at the pool itself.

Thundering sounds from the waterfall greeted our ears long before we arrived at the Butaweng River. Stopping near a bridge, we stood listening and staring at the sight each time. Up in the distance smaller falls tumbled over the rocks and into pools below them, and a wall of water from this level moved along to the edge of the bigger falls at the head of "our" pool. Mossy black rocks a thousand years old edged the pool, always covered with the ever-flowing water cleansing, cooling, and renewing itself.

During rainy season the river swelled to overflowing, creeping up over our narrow, slippery, rocky walkway, which led to the edge of our pool. The river's flow visibly increased in speed, relentlessly dragging along leaves, branches, small rocks, and debris. On such days we had to muster a lot of extra courage to jump in, especially since we always wanted to swim toward the falls, where the water was deepest. We gasped and panted as we swam long strokes against the current, aiming to duck around the side of the frothing water and clutch the rocky ledge behind the falls. From this vantage point we had a thundering view of the outside world, as seen through the clear wall of water. We trembled with fear and anticipation as we contemplated swimming back out to the world through the falls. Braver and younger members of our party liked to try swimming out right under the parts where the falls hit. Others of us, wiser and more fearful, crept back out via the edge of the wall of water. Some days there was no way to find a way around the foam, as the wall of water completely covered the whole width of the river. The water absolutely thundered as it poured over the rocky falls, and those who wanted to climb to the top of the falls and dive into the pool had to be especially foot sure, so that the water wouldn't trip them and send them hurtling onto the jagged rocks below.

One day when we gathered at the poolside, sitting on rocks and splashing our feet in the water, we heard a scream from near the falls. We dropped into the water and took long strokes across the pool to the waterfall, where our daughter, Heidi, was floating, trembling and sobbing. We guided her to the nearest rock, gently pushed her up onto the rock, and asked her what was wrong. She had jumped into the water at the base of the waterfall, but had jumped too close, and the tremendous power from the wall of water had caught her and pushed her deep into the pool, terrifying her. After panicking, she'd stopped fighting the pounding water and relaxed, and the water pushed her right out and she came up. She'd received a terrible scare, but at our gentle encouragement, she went back into the water that same day, swimming just for enjoyment away from the waterfall.

Several ancient rocks, largely submerged like icebergs, ringed the deepest part of the pool, and we liked to swim from rock to rock, clutching the crags and catching our breath before propelling ourselves off to the next crag.

Sunny mornings sharpened the breathtaking colors of our waterfall scene. The aquamarine water shimmered as though filled with jewels, while the sun shone through a canopy of immense trees framing the river. Sheets of clear water looked brown rolling over the dark rocks, turning to roiling white froth when crashing onto the water below, changing to dark aqua in the deepest section, and gradually lightening as it flowed along more shallow parts of the river, with brown patches over the rocky "icebergs."

The Butaweng River served as a social gathering place, a place where young and old, black, brown, and white, came together to wash, swim, shampoo, do the laundry, eat, discuss the world's problems, share jokes and stories, and contemplate the wonders of God's powerful, "water-full" creation. Unwritten but familiar rules governed the allowed activities designated for various sections of this river. Shallow pools of water between sheltering rocks offered safe wading pools for toddlers and for those who couldn't swim. A bit farther downriver, centuries-old water-chiseled rocks beckoned to be rubbed with soapy clothes, as families dragged bundles of clothing to the river to be washed. Within just a short distance, this renewing river easily cleansed the soapy water, for the water flowed over hundreds of rocks under the bridge nearby before tumbling down yet another huge waterfall. A bit upstream from the "laundry area" lay a couple of rocks with a smooth ledge—a perfect place to set soap and shampoo. After people had washed their hair, they dived into the clear water to rinse off the shampoo, and this sudsy water, too, swiftly vanished downstream to be purified over rocks. I often wondered how long it would be before the engineers of so-called progress and the business companies of "civilization" would barbarically rob this magnificent river of its healing, cleansing powers.

Meals at the Butaweng River were more like worship services than meals. Like a mighty organ recital, the water provided constant background music for our meal. To be sure, we brought food—maybe a casserole and salad, maybe some cooked ears of corn and home-baked rye bread sandwiches, and we brought lots of ice water and freshly squeezed lime juice. However, sitting on the steep, grassy bluff of this river valley, dangling our legs over the side, munching our food, and talking about a hundred different things, we constantly thrilled to the awesome power of that cascading wall of water. We talked about its source, about the froth, about our fears, and about its constancy. I thought about God's grace, which I often described as a gentle rain shower. Here this waterfall reminded me, not about the gentleness of God's grace, but about its majestic power to heal and cleanse. God's grace, like an unending sheet of water cascading over rocky falls, plunges into our lives and changes us forever. God's grace, like a river bubbling over hard, slippery rocks, flows over our hardened hearts, washing away debris of doubts and guilt caught in our brokenness, freeing us to become God's agents of forgiveness wherever we are.

Just like a waterfall can be dangerous, however, God's grace can be dangerous, too, when we abuse it. Grace's power cleanses us, but it also helps us to change the direction of our lives. Heidi learned a rather frightening lesson about the power of the waterfall that day when it pushed her into the depths of the river. We so easily take God's grace for granted, just like we easily forget about the miracle of water in our lives. Perhaps we abuse God's grace when we discount its power, when we say we forgive someone but we still bring up the subject over and over again, or when we are not willing to let this grace change our lifestyles.

During our picnics at the Butaweng River we always encountered other people, and we had special opportunities to interact with many different persons on such days. At this river community functioned powerfully. Mothers gently shampooed and bathed their toddlers; fathers guided their unsteady youngsters over slippery rocks into the pool; older siblings bounced their baby sisters and brothers up and down in the cooling water; neighbors merrily scrubbed their families' laundry on adjacent rounded rocks, talking and joking, their peals of laughter punctuating the roar of the waterfall. People learned about their neighbors' illnesses, deaths, and concerns. They discussed plantings and harvests; they planned trips to the store and the market; and they proudly watched their growing children gleefully shrieking as they threw themselves off the top of the falls into the water.

Yes, a picnic swim at the Butaweng was a celebration of life. Sitting there and eating, we felt like we gained access to the whole world—hearing a variety of languages, visiting with persons of many age groups and traditions and cultures, learning about a plethora of needs, and understanding anew the meaning of the word "community."

Where is our waterfall now to remind us of God's grace? Perhaps we don't have access to such a magnificent tropical pool. We do, however, have the privilege and the miracle of clean water, good water pressure in our showers, water fountains near some public buildings, and beautiful rivers within easy driving distance from most locations. As we go and sit by a powerful source of water, we can remember the power of God's grace in our lives.

fourteen

WHERE'S THE TOUGH FOOD?

"Good Morning. This is my niece. She should work for you. She should learn many things from you. She can start now. She will not cause you any trouble."

My mouth dropped open. Here stood a middle-aged woman from a nearby village, welcoming us to our new place of work by offering the help of her niece. I hadn't asked for anyone; in fact, I wasn't ready to employ a helper for the family. But this woman had known my parents. Her father had worked with my father many long years ago, and she herself had helped my folks when I was a child. Now, her niece was here to continue the tradition. Somewhat apprehensively and reluctantly, we agreed to try this arrangement.

Bumang helped our family in countless ways during the next years. She spent several hours of each day in our home, helping with the cooking, gardening, and babysitting, earning some money for her future, and learning about our good and not-so-good customs. During those years we often had guests who came by plane, ship, truck, car, and on foot from many different places. Every week we had visitors and guests on several days, and we cooked between thirty and sixty extra meals every month. Bumang's presence in our family became a tremendous blessing and a life saver for me.

One day a young man arrived to declare that he and Bumang would be married soon, and that they wanted us to be involved in the wedding. Her family planned joyful festivities, and soon the big day arrived. The wedding turned out to be a happy mixture of traditional and modern customs, and we enjoyed the celebrations together. Even though the newlyweds continued to live in our area, we didn't often have opportunities to visit together, so after their first son was born, we decided to invite the family of three for dinner after church one day.

Our Sunday worship services took place in a simple church building with walls about a yard high, leaving plenty of space between walls and iron roof for worshipers to catch a balmy tropical breeze, or to be sprinkled from some windblown rain. The best advantage of such a building was its view. We could look out on the green, green shrubs dotted with exotic, brilliantly colored hibiscus flowers; or we could gaze up at the dozens of flowering trees surrounding the church yard, while the breezes bore waves of fragrant perfumes toward us. Raising our eyes higher, we caught the breathtaking view of distant, majestic mountains capped with tufts of clouds heavy with rain.

Inside the building, hundreds of worshipers packed the long, sturdy pews, and when the pews were full, we spilled over onto the cement floor in the aisles and along the walls. Mothers sat cross-legged on the floor, cradling their infants, swaying as they lulled them to sleep with perfectly sterile breast milk. Older toddlers sat on their fathers' laps on the other side of the sanctuary, and school age children joined their family or relatives or other friends in the pews or out under the magnificent, shady trees. No sound system was needed for this church. The liturgists and preachers spoke loudly and clearly, their voices easily carrying to the back of the sanctuary and over the low walls to the ears of all those sitting outside.

Never will I forget the singing. Some Sundays the congregation sang so lustily, that overseas visitors would hold their ears in fright as the sound was too loud for them. Our congregation could sing hymn after hymn of praise to the Lord. They sang in their own language, often using folk melodies from their pre-Christian times. The verses of their hymns praised their creator God, their Redeemer, and reflected prayer and intercession.

During the singing our eyes followed the hymns in the hymnbook as we all joined in the lusty songs. During the readings, congregation members who could read followed the readings of the texts in their Bibles. People each carried a hymnal and a New Testament along to every service. When the complete Bible had been translated into their language, they bought a Bible and faithfully carried this, together with the hymnal, over the muddy trails, through the forests, or over slippery logs crossing the streams. In a land where every book is precious and expensive, these two books were sometimes the only books in the house.

Many of our neighbors carefully wrapped their two books in a large cotton handkerchief and then laid them into a string carrying bag or tucked this package under one arm as they walked to church. These books might also shelter a birth certificate, a baptism certificate, or some precious photographs.

On this particular Sunday morning, as always, we worshiped together in the church. I hurried home after the service to cook our dinner. Our family would number seven persons for dinner, since Bumang's family of three would join our family of four. I oven-fried a precious chicken—a favorite meat in Papua New Guinea but quite expensive to buy—and planned to serve fried rice and vegetables with the chicken.

At noon we looked through the louvers and noticed our guests arriving.

"How many people are you expecting?" asked Ron.

"Just three," I returned.

"What about all those others with them?" he queried.

"Oh, they are probably just visiting after meeting on the road."

We went to the door and opened it to welcome our friends. They walked in, and behind them came some of their relatives. Soon more arrived, and then even more. Soon we numbered seventeen persons, and everyone found a place to sit—some on chairs, some on the sofa, and some on the floor. An air of excitement and anticipation shone on every face. My face registered utter panic as I slipped into the kitchen and tore open my cupboard doors, panting stressfully. *What can I quickly cook to feed this crowd?* The nearest grocery store was far away, and the nearest fast food restaurant was a hundred miles away; besides, there wasn't a road leading there anyway. Our current garden yielded delicate sprays of exotic orchids, sweet-smelling, waxy frangipani flowers, and thousands of purple bougainvillea blossoms, but no vegetables.

I looked at the forlorn little chicken pieces in my oven, crunchy and smelling scrumptious. I wondered whether this was a good time to reflect on the way five loaves and two fishes fed a crowd of thousands two millennia ago. I said a quick prayer, rapidly cut each piece into smaller pieces, and proceeded to make a big amount of gravy. Into the gravy went some chopped onion and a couple of cans of tomatoes. Canned tomatoes were one luxury item we permitted ourselves every time we went on our once-every-three-months grocery shopping trips to Lae, a seven-hour boat journey away. We bought fresh vegetables and fruit directly from villagers, but tomatoes did not grow well in our area, due to torrential rains and insect pests. The larder revealed some packets of spaghetti, so my big saucepan was soon bubbling with boiling water and spaghetti. Another pot with a few hastily pared sweet potatoes, topped with a couple of bunches of fresh spinach, joined the boiling food on our stove. Meanwhile, we poured fresh lime juice over ice cubes for all—a deliciously refreshing drink on a hot day. Lively conversation ensued while dinner was expanding in our kitchen. Soon everything was ready, and we wondered whether we could make the food stretch.

Our oldest guest was a feisty and outspoken old aunt of Bumang. While the others eagerly accepted the different foods we served them, Auntie flatly turned down my offer of spaghetti. I knew that she had a number of teeth missing, so I thought it would be good for her to have the soft food. However, she protested, saying that if she'd eat soft food, her remaining teeth would get loose and fall out. She gave us a sound lecture about the perils and foolishness of eating soft food. In spite of this, however, we enjoyed a good visit together; besides, everyone had food to eat after all, and a cheerful atmosphere prevailed.

After our company family left, we chuckled over the aunt's protests. We'd not thought before about the ways tough steak and hard corn prevented our teeth from weakening and falling out, even though we knew a lot of chewing was good for our gums. Moreover, we knew dogs strengthened their teeth by chewing on bones and other hard items such as table legs and oak trimmings in a house. This lesson also reminded us of the words in the Bible about solid spiritual food necessary for mature believers.

Auntie and her big family had gently taught us another lesson, namely, the tremendous importance of the extended family in this culture. Our years of serving overseas, thousands of miles from most of our extended family members, taught us to treasure our friendships with neighbors and coworkers, who stepped in as family on many occasions, enriching our lives, just as Bumang and her family did, in unexpected ways.

fifteen

MEALS ON THE MOVE

"Tomorrow we're going to Wau! Tomorrow we're going to Wau!" sang Natalie and Graham jubilantly, as we scrambled to pack together our bags. We could hardly wait to go to visit our daughter, Heidi, who attended the boarding school at Wau.

Finally, "tomorrow" came. Between completing a dozen final errands on the station, we took turns watching the ocean for signs of the little ship which would transport us on the first leg of our journey. At last, it came into view from the north, a regal white vessel bobbing up and down in the glistening aquamarine sea. We passed the word around, grabbed our bags and our packed lunches and bottles of water, and clambered aboard the waiting truck. Thirty minutes later, we arrived at the wharf and joined the queues of people lined up in front of the miniscule ticket booth. After our ship berthed, we had to wait patiently for passengers to disembark and for cargo to be unloaded. Sometimes that took many hours, while at other times the turn-around took a very brief time.

After what seemed an interminable time, we were aboard, making ourselves as comfortable as possible on the narrow bunks, sharing news with friends and strangers in adjoining bunks, and nibbling a snack before lying down to await the first big heaves of the waves outside the sheltered harbor area. Once we became accustomed to the gently rolling ship, we ventured up again and sat up reading, talking, and watching for playful porpoises frolicking alongside the boat. In the distance, the ever-changing coastline, back-dropped by blue, jungle-clad mountains, provided endlessly exquisite tropical vistas for our eyes. At times, however, a quick rush to the railing to involuntarily feed the fish interrupted the view-gazing.

Seven hours later, around dusk, the city of Lae came into view, and soon the ship was cutting its engines and gliding into Lae harbor. Staying overnight in Lae was never a hardship for us in those years, for we had Grandma there, who welcomed us into a beautifully clean little house, crisp new sheets on her guest beds, and delicious foods from her kitchen. We relaxed and caught up on town news, while Natalie and Graham played contentedly with the toys from my mother's hall closet.

Early next morning, we found a ride to a public bus stop and stood waiting for a bus to take us on to Wau. Soon a bus arrived. I passed up the first one, because it featured so many dents, that I wondered whether the driver had a drinking problem. Soon another bus arrived and pulled in to the hot, dusty stop. Since I was traveling alone with two little ones, I wanted to make sure I would not be left stranded anywhere on the way, so I first went to the driver's window and had a little chat with him.

"Good morning. Is this bus going all the way to Wau today?"

"Yes, Mama," he replied between chews of betel nut.

"Will you be the driver all the way?"

"Yes, Mama, this is my bus and I am the driver."

"Do you have room for me and my two little ones?"

"Yes, we do," he replied, waving magnanimously to the hordes of passengers behind his seat and shouting at them to make room for Mama and her little ones.

"Thank you," I said, "And when we get to Wau, where will you drop us off?"

"Mama, I will take you all the way up the hill to the school and drop you off right in front of the school," he promised.

"And will we get there before dark?" was my next question.

"Yes, we always get there before dark."

"My husband is not with me today. Will I be safe in this bus all the way?" I persisted.

"Yes, I promise you will be safe, Mama." Then, turning around, he shouted, "Are you going to help look after this mama and her babies?" and the whole, crowded busload waved and shouted in reply, "Yes, sure we will."

And they did.

Gleefully we climbed in and stumbled along the narrow aisle which was heavily packed with string bags, hands of bananas, bundles of coconuts, pet dogs, and one squealing piglet in a bag. We found a space between two generous fellow passengers, with Graham perched on my lap and Natalie next to me on the seat. I crammed bags under the seat and took out a sturdy plastic sack (just in case someone would get carsick), adjusted myself, and began to look around me, greeting my new, smiling traveling companions. The children and I formed a very pale patch of humanity in a sea of cheerful dark brown faces.

We roared out of Lae, leaving behind a trail of dust and some very dust-filled faces at the bus stop, and no sooner had we settled down when the bus lurched to a screeching stop. I asked, "What's the matter?"

They replied, "We are picking up some more passengers." I was incredulous. The bus was absolutely full to my well-trained Western eyes. But in Papua New Guinea there is always room for more. Cheerfully, we made room for a few more passengers there at that stop, and a couple miles out of town we stopped again and picked up a few more. I kept thinking, *In spite of all the stops, at least we are moving in the direction of Wau.*

Slowly the bus began to climb as the road twisted and turned around the mountains. On either side of the road grew thick shrubs and trees; soon, the elegant coconut trees in the lowlands gave way to flowering trees and other timbers, as we began gaining altitude along the dusty road. Our bus puffed and panted whenever we ascended steeper slopes, but it nevertheless kept going. The journey from Lae to Wau took anywhere from four to six hours, depending on the age of the vehicle, the weather, the passengers, and impediments along the way. Closer to Wau we wound through beautiful gorges, following the course of a mountain river snaking its way down the ranges hundreds of feet below us along the side of our narrow road. For passengers not familiar with the road, the ride could be a bit of a harrowing experience. I kept comforting myself with the knowledge that our driver knew every inch of the road, since he made this journey every day.

Between admiring the virgin jungle views outside the window, we began visiting with our amiable fellow passengers, who seemed delighted that we could converse with them in Melanesian Pidgin. We talked about home villages, family members, purposes for travel, and some of the latest news. Between our conversations, other groups of persons spoke animatedly and cheerfully in their own languages. The chatter in several different languages was so much a part of our lives, that we really didn't notice how many different languages we could hear. However, it struck me again how quickly these total strangers "adopted" our family, and how quickly we became friends. As always, our children bonded instantly with theirs.

Presently, we reached the roads near the town of Bulolo, which had been a bustling mining town in the late 1930's. Now, huge carcasses of cumbersome gold dredges lay rusting in dried out river beds in the area, like abandoned dinosaurs of an earlier age, nestled among millions of small pebbles thrown up out of river beds and dumped on the surrounding hillsides. Among these mounds, village men and women had valiantly tried to plant their gardens; however, the mining processes had damaged the land irreparably, and good, arable land had become scarce.

How easily colonizers denuded precious forest land in many parts of the world in the name of progress and civilization. Sometimes our Western bringing of "civilization" to so-called "primitive people" seemed more like barbarism compared to the communal, cooperative, subsistence life styles which so many of these people carried out before the times of "progress." True, fear and superstition and fighting had been part of many cultures, but this was no excuse for explorers and businessmen and colonizers to rupture and destroy fragile communal culture systems. Viewing many acres of stripped land on this journey brought me a somber reminder of mining's destruction in the world.

We were heading down a long, steep mountain when suddenly the bus swung to the side of the road, lurched, and wheezed to a halt. I glanced anxiously at my new friends, and they fired off some questions at the driver. A strange burning stench permeated the bus, and we wondered whether we should flee. Our driver jumped out, grabbed a couple of big plastic bottles, told us to stay where we were, and he and a couple of other men disappeared down over the edge of the road to the valley below. Thinking they went to relieve themselves, I sat back and tried to relax. A few minutes later the men reappeared, lugging the bottles which were now filled with water from a stream below. They threw the bottles of water at the wheels which sizzled with steam, and we realized that the brakes had overheated on the long downward stretch of road. Soon we were on our way again.

Presently, our companions pulled out some snacks to nibble and immediately offered us some. One woman had a couple of ears of cooked corn, while another brought out a cucumber; one woman held a firm, yellow banana; another, wielding a large pointed knife, deftly poked a hole into a fresh coconut, so that all could share in its refreshing drink. By this time, the children were really hungry, so we, too, pulled out our crackers and sandwiches and fruit. Our fellow passengers offered us some of their food, and we offered them some of ours. An impromptu potluck lunch took place right then and there as we bobbed up and down in that instant community builder, the bus.

Daytime gave way to dusk as we rounded the final ninety corners between the little towns of Bulolo and Wau. By this time, we were all getting anxious to arrive at our destination and stretch our cramped legs. Natalie and Graham sang excitedly as their eyes strained at every corner for a glimpse of the school. Finally, our trusty bus dropped into a lower gear for the final hill right at the entrance to Katharine Lehmann School. It roared up the hill and stopped abruptly at the top. Passengers gently shoved us toward the door, handing me baby and bags, shouting cheerful farewells and greetings as we gingerly stepped down. I paid the driver on the way out—a custom there—and thanked him and his "boats crew," the title given to the man in the front seat next to the driver. He collected the money and helped with any administrative decisions, should some arise.

We were on firm ground again. We waved at our travel companions as the bus lurched forward and sped down the hill, turned right, and headed into the town of Wau to drop off the rest of the load of people. With shrieks of delight the children saw Heidi approaching to greet us, and soon we were trooping off to the guest house, all jabbering at once, and very glad to be together again.

Our visits to Wau gave us brief respites from the busyness of our tasks at home, and we relished these precious times, first with Joy and later with Heidi when they were attending school there. During meal times the children ate at the same table as their visiting family members, and that gave us a sense of being family again around the table, even if for only a few days at a time. We also visited with staff members and met other parents and visitors to Wau, learning about their work and lives. In addition, the spring-like climate up in the mountains re-energized us for our return to work at the steamy hot coast.

sixteen

TABLES OF GRACE

When the church's bishop asked us to move from our beloved Finschhafen to the city of Lae to help out at church headquarters, we were full of excitement and anticipation. Our children had reached favorable ages for a move to a town with international schools, and both Ron and I looked forward to new challenges in ministry. However, we knew that we were leaving behind many friends plus a house which boasted a million-dollar view over the Pacific, complete with breathtaking coral reefs, magnificent beaches, and incomparable sunrises, as well as a garden bursting with spectacular tropical orchids and cream roses.

For me the farewells in Finschhafen marked the end of a long chapter in my family's history, for this had been the place of my father's birth as well as my own. My grandparents had first gone to Finschhafen in 1906, and, despite many years of absence because of war, studies, and other family circumstances, our family had a deep-rooted connection with this little part of the world.

Finally we had completed our packing and said our farewells, loaded our goods on the boat, and traveled to our new home and new lives in the city of Lae. For years we had been visiting Lae to get groceries, attend meetings, and visit my parents. My father had died in Lae in 1968, and my mother had retired to Australia in 1981 and had died there in 1982. Moving to Lae a few months after her death brought us new and different perspectives of the city.

A blur of emotions filled us as we walked into our new home, scrubbed more than two hundred glass louvers which filled the windows, washed black mold off walls and ceilings, and began to unpack. Soon our treasured but somewhat faded pictures lent familiarity to the bare walls, the cupboards filled up, and we began to explore our environs, especially the spacious new yard bordering the forest at the edge of the city. Bird songs chorused us awake long before daylight every morning, while roosters often seemed to herald the arrival of a new day by looking at the street lights at midnight instead of waiting for dawn to break.

Ron went to work immediately in his new job, and I suddenly felt quite lost in our new surroundings. Within a couple of days, a new friend arrived to invite us to a potluck and Bible study in her home that Friday evening. I was thrilled and could hardly wait for Friday to come.

Our family went and discovered some familiar faces among the folk who gathered that Friday evening. Some families came with small, eager children, while other families included teenagers. Several single women and men came, too. Many of these participants were expatriate people from the USA, Australia, Germany, the Philippines, and Canada, working in missions or in business or agriculture. We squeezed into the tiny living room area of these new friends, finding a place to sit—a chair, a sofa, the floor, or a mat. We piled our food on their kitchen counter, unpacked our dishes and silverware, and paused briefly to sing a table grace—a song of thanks. Immediately, the noise and clatter began in earnest as all queued up, piled food on their plates, grabbed a glass of icy cold lemonade, and planted themselves somewhere to balance a plate on their knees and eat. Soon everyone was munching food in between stories and chuckles of laughter. We shared news and views with those sitting next to us, and quickly realized that we now lived in a very diverse community. People hailed not only from many different countries, but also from differing religious backgrounds, and I wondered how this Bible study would really go.

Well, it went, and it went well. First, a few people scrambled to collect dirty dishes and haul them into the kitchen, where willing men gathered for their ritual of dish-washing. None of our homes had dishwashers, and for these potlucks the men usually washed dishes. Kettles of water boiled away on the gas stove in readiness for the dishwashing routine, and soon loud laughter pealed over the clattering of dishes in the sink. By the time the crew emerged from the kitchen, we'd arranged chairs, floor pillows, and mats in as much of a circle as possible, and soon someone handed out songbooks, someone else grabbed a guitar, and we sang and sang. The children enjoyed this part of the program, too, joining in lustily and choosing many of the songs.

After much enthusiastic singing, someone said a prayer, and we opened our Bibles and had a short Bible study. This involved a time of discussion, in the whole group or sometimes in pairs or small groups, and we ended the study with a time of sharing prayer concerns and praying about them. A brief moment ensued, where someone volunteered to host the event two weeks from that night and someone else volunteered to lead the Bible study. Thus the evening ended, with tired but happy people gathering up their empty dishes and Bibles, chorusing "Goodnight," and heading for home.

Our Friday night Bible studies took place every two weeks and helped us to feel welcome in our new community in a very special way. Most of us women and men were working full time there in Lae, so we were often very tired by Friday night. Consequently, I often wondered whether we wouldn't be better off resting at home. Something, however, drew us to this group, and we hated to miss a session. Besides, we always came home renewed, and we found that this event became a priority in our lives.

As our children grew older, we thought they might get bored with this custom, and we gave them the freedom to decide to come along or go somewhere else or stay at home. Most of the time, they chose to come along, and I often observed special ways in which the younger children interacted with older adults during such evenings. The kids weren't shunted away into a corner even though they frequently chose the option of playing in another room during the actual Bible study time.

People enriched us by the variety of background experiences which they shared, not only through their food and religious insights, but also through their songs. Often we had guests staying with us on a Friday night; we invited them to come along with us, and invariably, they enjoyed meeting this community and sharing with them. There was always room for a few new friends and travelers. Many times the event took place in our house, which had a fairly large living room. Even when we met in very small homes, however, everyone somehow fitted in, and we quickly learned that the size of the house didn't matter nearly as much as the willingness of its residents.

Other potlucks took place for a variety of reasons. Often, such events served as extended family events, since most of us had no relatives living closer than thousands of miles from where we lived. As Americans living abroad, we often had to work on United States national holidays such as Memorial Day, Labor Day, Thanksgiving Day, and Independence Day. Instead of celebrating on these days, we took vacations on such hallowed days as the Queen's Birthday, Anzac Day (April 25), Good Friday, Easter Monday, and Boxing Day (December 26), when no stores would dare to open their doors. Occasionally, we USA people planned a celebration potluck on Thanksgiving Day or the Friday evening of Thanksgiving weekend. We then invited some non-Americans to join us, for many of us were a mixture of nationalities by birth or through marriage; besides, we weren't interested in promoting one-nationality exclusivity. Turkeys were prohibitively expensive, so we settled for chicken and other meats instead of turkey, until the year some folks came from Michigan and insisted we have proper turkey. Well, we all chipped in and spent almost 30 dollars to purchase a frozen turkey weighing about 10 pounds. One of us became the designated turkey cook, while others prepared various other dishes. We all got to sample the turkey, and it tasted delicious.

A typical accompaniment to a potluck gathering at Thanksgiving or Christmas was a swim, for Christmas was, after all, the hottest time of the year in the southern hemisphere. While we lived in Finschhafen, we had a choice of several magnificent beaches or rivers to cool us off after a sumptuous meal. In Lae the beaches were not as inviting nor as clean, but we sometimes had membership at a school pool and were allowed to book the pool for special occasions. Occasionally, we ate together at someone's house first and then piled into vehicles for the drive to a swimming place; at other times we took the potluck to the beach and ate there together.

Special potluck times occurred when the staff and faculty families of Balob Teachers College, where I taught for seven years, gathered on the college grounds for a shared meal. Such events often took place at the beginning or end of a school year and helped us to celebrate community in special ways. Since we faculty and staff members came from many parts of Papua New

Guinea as well as several other countries of the world, a potluck included delicious and sometimes mysterious dishes from a great variety of cultural backgrounds—a true ethnic feast, to say the least.

Often we shared a meal outdoors in our yard, and these provided special opportunities to eat and share harmony with nature—to admire the luxuriant greenery and a gala of tropical flowers around us. One memorable Sunday afternoon, about ninety of us—Papua New Guineans, Americans, Germans, Canadians, Australians, and others—gathered in our back yard for a wonderful potluck dinner, and when it was over, we formed a huge circle, sitting on the soft green grass, framed by hibiscus hedges, with a perfect backdrop of enormous vine-covered jungle trees. There we held a communion service, awed to be experiencing first-hand the Body of Christ, celebrating our diversity in special ways as well as the miracle of life all around us.

seventeen

MIDNIGHT MOURNING

A regular Friday night feature on our street in Lae was neighborhood worship when our neighbors, Sakey and Nancy, hosted evening devotions for children and others in the neighborhood. With our windows invariably wide open to catch every refreshing breath of air on sultry tropical evenings, we loved to hear these sounds of joyful voices accompanied by guitars. Not only the participants benefited from these evenings, but also neighbors, passers by, and out-of-town visitors could share in the celebrations, whether sitting in the yard among the participants or not. Children, adolescents, singles, and couples gathered in the yard, sitting on logs or on the grass as they worshiped, prayed, and visited together under the starry tropical sky. Even when the sky gave way to torrents of tropical rains, the singing continued, albeit a bit muffled, for the group had to squeeze into the tiny rooms of the house to shelter from the rain.

One day Erao, their son, became ill. His parents and teachers had noticed that he was developing problems with remembering things at school. Every day he became worse, and one day he went into a coma, and had to be hospitalized. Doctors tried in vain to establish the diagnosis. His parents and other relatives kept a constant vigil at his side. Erao's father and mother both had full-time jobs, but his mother, who was a school teacher, took a leave of absence for a term in order to care for her son. Grandfather, uncles, aunts, and cousins made the long journey from their home villages to take their turn at Erao's bed in hospital. They stayed there night and day. They cooked and brought liquid broth, vegetable broth, and milk, which the nurses fed to him through a tube that went through his mouth and his nose. They spoke to him, prayed with him, told him what was going on in their lives, and bathed him lovingly each day.

Meantime, back at home, the Friday night worship times continued. Erao would have wanted that. He had been active and regular at Sunday school and worship, and his last conscious outing was to Sunday school down the road. On that Sunday he spoke with his friends at Sunday school, and after that he did not speak again.

One morning a message came from hospital to say the family should hurry and come, for Erao had taken a turn for the worse. A few hours later he passed away. The family brought his body back to the house and began to make preparations for his funeral.

Word of Erao's death spread like a fast wind, and soon people began to gather from all over the country to mourn the death of this happy eleven-year-old. Neighbors, school friends, and teachers joined the family members, not just for a day or two, but for a week or two. Relatives arrived in truckloads from distant mountain villages, and each fresh group of arrivals triggered a new outbreak of lament. Often a truckload of people arrived around midnight, after a long, bumpy, exhausting journey from Erao's mother's mountainous home area of Chimbu Province. People piled out, hugging the family members and weeping. Some ran to rub ashes or clay onto their bodies—a ritual symbolizing grief; others arrived already covered with red clay. Even though their crying sounded harsh and almost angry at first, it gradually gave way to a chant-like lament. Gradually, the crying turned into hymn-singing. Mourners began to chant hymns of hope and petition. An occasional loud sob or sigh punctuated the singing, which gradually waned and then ceased. With soothing murmurs, mothers cradled their nursing infants and shifted positions on the ground, while toddlers snuggled against a parent or sibling or another relative. Some sat up leaning against one another, while others draped loin cloths around themselves, curled up, and lay down on the ground. Soon tropical night sounds such as the chirping of crickets and the hooting of owls replaced the sounds of mourning. Pet dogs stepped among the now-relaxed mass of sleeping bodies, sniffing the ground for food morsels.

This interlude was short-lived, however, for around two o'clock in the morning, dull thuds of an axe chopping wood broke through the damp night air. Someone started a big cooking fire in the yard, and women began to peel sweet potatoes. A young man grabbed an axe and split some coconuts. The time came for readying some food. Women dragged pots out of the house and filled them with water. Some of the yams went into the pot, while others went in among the hot coals flanking the fire's flames. Once again, occasional wails of grief interspersed with hymns of lament rose into the night air together with the smoke from the fires.

Soon the food was ready. No table was large enough to accommodate everyone, but they ate, laughed, talked, and then lay down wherever they were, and slept for a while. All too quickly dawn would break for another day, and then the crying and singing would begin all over again.

Those weeks our neighbors and their friends and families witnessed to us in powerful ways. Occasionally, we joined the mourners in the yard for their evening worship times, just to sit with them, to meditate, and to be in community with them. Often, however, we just participated from a distance. For several weeks we had very little sleep with all of this activity happening just a few yards from our bedroom windows. However, every morning we left for work and school refreshed and renewed in special ways. For me it was an intense time for reflection about life and death, a time of recognizing the therapeutic value of grieving "with hope." I struggled with my own fears of death, and with my disappointment that this young lad had died so young in spite of the prayers of many persons in the community. I tried to imagine myself in his mother's position, coping with the death of her son, and the thoughts led to feelings of anger and fear.

I marveled at the way eating together as community broke barriers and provided pauses in our grieving, allowing laughter to punctuate our sorrow. At first I was worried that the noises from our house would interfere with our neighbor family's mourning, and I tried to tell our own children and their friends, as well as our guests, to keep as quiet as possible. Yet when we heard the rowdy, happy, normal life sounds which came from our neighbors between their bouts of weeping, we knew that they accepted our normal sounds in the same way.

I thought back to the time when my own father died, there in the same city of Lae, when friends came by at all hours to cry a little with us, to sit with us, and to be a community with us. Mother would go to the kitchen after a while and would prepare a snack for us to share, and through the tears we broke into smiles, sharing the life gifts of food, sharing other family news, and being normal. So life goes on, and death continues to be part of life.

Friday night worship continued. Children, youth, singles, and couples dropped whatever they were doing, and came from around the compound to lift their voices in thanks and praise to the Lord of Hope. None of us will ever be quite the same again, thanks to the witness of these precious neighbors who taught us anew what it means to be part of the Body of Christ.

eighteen

CROCODILE IN STYLE

One afternoon I took my teachers' college students on a class excursion to the crocodile farm. This was a new experience for all of us, and as I drove the truck with the precious load of 25 college students out of town along the winding road, I wondered what such a farm would be like. We reached the area and piled out of the truck. We entered the farm, and the guide showed us some of the 35,000 young crocodiles which were raised there for their skins, since wealthy ladies and gentlemen of the United States of America and other countries still prized items made from crocodile skin.

Just as we were ready to return to the college, one of the students spotted a relative of his working in the skinning room. An ecstatic reunion followed, and we all had to wait for him to complete his formalities with his cousin. When we were ready, the cousin and his workmates offered us a couple of three-foot long skinned crocodiles to take back with us. We grinned at each other in disbelief, hesitated for a moment, and then eagerly accepted the gifts. Within a couple of minutes we were in the truck again, heading back to campus with 25 students, two teachers, and two skinned crocodiles.

On the way back the students were excited about the meat, for their diet at school was very short on meat. They decided to freeze and save the crocodiles for our class party, which was to take place in a few days' time. Slowly, however, doubt began to take the place of enthusiasm, for none of us had ever eaten a crocodile, much less prepared and cooked one. When we arrived back at the college, a lively discussion ensued. Was the meat really edible? Were there any taboos connected with eating such meat? The Seventh Day Adventist students immediately said there was no way they could eat this meat, since it belonged to the "creeping and crawling" category of things forbidden in their religion. The group then agreed to cook some other meat, too, so that these students would not be left out. We decided to meet after classes the next day in order to plan our class party.

Meanwhile, I went home and scanned the recipe books. None of them—not even Betty Crocker's Cookbook, my old standby—yielded a recipe for crocodile. My friends tried to be helpful. An Australian friend said she had a recipe for kangaroo tail soup and one for witchetty grubs; a doctor's wife from the USA said she had a recipe for flying fox in plum sauce; another knew how to barbecue eel; but none had cooked a crocodile. Finally, we received some practical hints from another friend who had cooked and eaten crocodile meat and had lived to tell the story. We decided to go ahead with our plans.

At our meeting the next day, the students carefully planned the budget for buying the food for the feast. Some of them went to the huge open air market for fresh greens, taro, sweet potatoes, and yams, as well as delicious tropical fruits. Others went to the grocery store to purchase such items as bread, ketchup, chicken (for those who would not touch crocodile), as well as some margarine and ice cream.

Saturday dawned, and the students came over to our house early to dig shallow pits in the back yard. They lined the pits with smooth round stones, filled them with wood, kindled the wood, and covered the piles with more stones. Next, they spread long green banana leaves over everything and tossed loose earth over them to keep in the heat. These stones would become red hot in order to bake the food which we planned to put into the pits.

Students who came from the Rabaul area on New Britain Island supervised the preparations as the food was going to cook in the "islands *mumu*" style. They peeled and washed the sweet potatoes and taro; then they washed and prepared the greens, onions, and pumpkin pieces. Walen, one of the most nimble students, scaled a tall coconut tree in our yard and knocked down some green coconuts for drinking tangy, refreshing, clear coconut water. They broke open several brown coconuts which had fallen from the trees earlier, and they grated the rich soft, snow-white flesh. This grated flesh they then squeezed through a clean cloth, yielding thick, creamy coconut milk. The young women poured this creamy milk over the pieces of meat and vegetables neatly piled on "sheets" of banana leaves. Next, they deftly wrapped the leaves around the food, and each little bundle was then ready for the *mumu*.

Since the heated stones were also ready by now, students cleaned away the ashes from the burnt wood and gently set the bundles of food into the pits. One pit had bundles with crocodile pieces; the other pit had bundles which contained chicken pieces with the vegetables. The young men carefully piled hot stones on top of the bundles, poured water on the hot stones, and covered the piles with more banana leaves. Finally, they shoveled dirt over everything.

As the food steamed and cooked away between the hot stones, smoke tendrils oozed their way out and up into the air, soon to be accompanied by a wonderful smell. Meanwhile, some of us busied ourselves upstairs in the kitchen, preparing fresh salad foods and fruit platters for the meal. Others sat under the magnificent tall trees in the yard, strumming at a couple of guitars, singing, telling stories, and crying, too, for this was graduation week. Soon they would be scattered all over the country, teaching in community schools dotted in remote areas of this beautiful, rugged land. Their two years at teachers' college were almost over. Two years ago they had arrived unsure, frightened to be among so many strangers, and insecure about many things. They formed lasting friendships with students from other areas of the country—sometimes even with students of traditional enemy tribes. How would life continue for them now after leaving the security of dormitory and campus life?

Late afternoon turned into a steamy tropical dusk, and evening turned into night with amazing rapidity. The sun vanished behind the rugged blue jungle-covered mountains on the horizon, and up and down the street came the sounds of an axe chopping into wood, women banging pots and pans, and hungry children scurrying around, laughing as they played or crying as they clamored for food. People ambled up the road from the main street, carrying their market supplies in the *bilums,* sturdy string bags woven from the fibers of the leaves of a cactus-like plant. Dogs sniffed about, lingering around the fires and hunting for morsels of food.

Our yard buzzed with activity and anticipation. Students carefully removed the dirt and outer leaves from over the pits. Next, they deftly lifted away the hot stones by means of two long sticks. Gingerly, they lifted out the precious bundles of food, carrying them to a table which we'd spread with fresh banana leaves. They opened the bundles and spread out the food. We had plates and forks ready, for now the feast was prepared.

All of us dragged mats and stools in a big circle around the table. After a prayer of thanks and some words of welcome, we filed around the table and filled our plates. We took the plates and sat down on our big circle. We took a bite. It tasted delicious. We laughed with relief as we dug in for more good food and sat cross-legged on the mats. After the meal we sang some songs, accompanied by guitars and an uninvited mosquito chorus. Between songs we shared special farewell messages of encouragement with one another. I shared verses from the letter of Philippians in the Bible, with reminders about the importance of maintaining their joyfulness and their thankfulness even in difficult times, and their trust in God's gift of peace.

As we lingered together in our circle that evening, we realized that this risk of trying a new kind of food drew us together in a special way. I couldn't help wondering what other "crocodiles" these young people would encounter in their lives: new customs in areas where they were assigned to teach, unusual traditions, new ways of worship, and political or physical or mental crises. Their lives, just like our lives, often included an element of risk. We knew we needed to branch out sometimes and dare to try something new—not only new food, but new ways to reach out to others.

nineteen

STEPS ALONG THE WARIA RIVER

A Day during our Ten-Day School-visiting Patrol

Our host village began to stir soon after four o'clock in the morning, but no one seemed to be up and about until around six. By six-thirty Ron and I were up and packed. Angry red bites covered my body, and they itched terribly. Obviously, the mosquitoes and sand flies had had a good meal yesterday, probably just before we had crawled under our mosquito nets and into our sleeping bags. We suspected some smaller insects often found their way through the nets, too.

At seven Ron went over to the village school house, which was built entirely of jungle materials. He spent the next three hours observing lessons, discussing various matters with the teacher, and making out his report. Children and teacher interacted enthusiastically during lessons despite the appalling lack of equipment in this remote educational establishment. With about thirty-six local school children, the school provided vital literacy skills for families. I went along and watched classes for about an hour, but then I went back through the village and ended up joining a group of women sitting around a fire in their bamboo-and-grass house. They couldn't speak either of the two Papua New Guinea languages which I could speak, but we carried on a most animated conversation, complete with arm-waving, laughter, and lots of sign language.

Nearby, several women prepared lunch for our group. They scraped the skin of big taro tubers, peeled them swiftly and efficiently with a long sharp knife, deftly cut them into large chunks, and dropped them into a large round pot full of water. Another pot filled with chicken pieces and sliced onions bubbled away over a smoky fire alongside the cooking hut. A young girl split some coconuts with a machete and collected its refreshing water into a tin bowl. Then, sitting cross-legged on a grating stool, she kept rubbing the inner part of the coconut around the grater, and I watched as a snowy pile of grated coconut grew in the bowl below the grater. The girl spooned bunches of the grated coconut onto the center of a clean cotton cloth, gathered the ends and joined them at the top, then twisted the ends and squeezed as thick, rich, white coconut cream oozed out of the cloth. She poured this cream over some golden boiling pumpkin pieces. Steam from these pots carried a tantalizing aroma, and I hoped Ron would soon be back from school so that we could eat. For us it was a special day, for we were having lunch for the first time in six days. We usually made up for it by eating big breakfasts and evening meals.

Presently our group was sitting in a circle on bamboo mats on the floor of our guest house, eating chicken, taro, and pumpkin pieces in coconut milk. I wasn't sure what to call this meal: was it breakfast or brunch or lunch? Whatever its name, it tasted delicious. We could tell from the position of the sun that it was time to get moving, and soon we were on our way, after many handshakes, expressions of thanks, and goodbyes.

After walking for almost three hours, we arrived at a bend in the river, where a canoe, carved from the trunk of a large hardwood tree, lay waiting to carry us for the remainder of the day's journey in sheer luxury. We clambered aboard, gingerly positioning ourselves and our bags on the outrigger in such a way that we could hang our feet into the dugout part of the canoe. Our guide perched at the back of this canoe, his wide flat oar slicing the chocolate-colored water first on one side, then on the other, and this way we made our way downstream.

Our downstream glide on the water offered us a panorama of the banks, with virgin forest hugging both sides of the river. This was luxury compared to the previous week's trekking that had taken us upstream along this large river. Shrieking white cockatoos mocked us as they darted in and out among the trees, and brilliant butterflies flitted in and out among the flowering shrubs close to the river's banks. Soon we arrived at Mou village, and after greeting the villagers, we decided to have an early bath in the river there, which looked a little less opaque than the Waria River.

We bathed with our clothes on, since the river was a very public place. Ron went to a section of the river where men bathed, while I went to a part where women bathed. While I was soaping my body, one woman casually mentioned that she hadn't seen "the crocodile" there yet today. I leaped out of the water in panic, running up the bank as far away from any crocodiles as possible. I was very relieved that we didn't see one. Later, we sat in the guest house made of woven palms and grass thatch. As we chatted with the people, they showed us the huge long snout of a sawfish they'd caught in the ocean earlier. Its saw-like snout measured almost three feet in length, and it had very sharp teeth on both sides. By evening the whole village was cooking fish for dinner, for there was enough of this enormous sea animal to go around. After all, without refrigeration, the best thing to do was to cook and enjoy any fish as soon after catching it as possible.

We wondered what sawfish would taste like, and we soon found out. The fish tasted somewhat tough and had a rather strong flavor, resembling shark meat, but we ate some pieces and found it delicious with the accompanying vegetables.

After our meal we joined the villagers for their customary evening vespers in the village chapel, a tradition practiced in hundreds of villages throughout the country. Our hosts invited Ron to lead the service, and following that we sat around on the porch of the house, while village children provided entertainment for everyone on this wonderfully balmy evening. The center of the village was bare and sandy, with twenty-five houses constructed around in the shape of a large oval. Here the children performed graceful dances, awkwardly funny mimes, and entertaining skits. We joined their parents, laughing and clapping at their antics, and we felt honored to be accepted as part of the family here. Many of the children wore grass skirts not made from traditional jungle string, but from the twine of rice bags which they'd frayed to within a few inches from the top. They could slip these "bags" on, tie them at their waists, and the result looked quite impressive.

Presently, children needed to get ready for bed, and adults began to disperse, too, so with a chorus of goodnights we, too, decided to retire for the evening. Unrolling our sleeping bag and positioning our crumpled mosquito net once again, we surveyed our skin and noticed that not much spare space remained on our skins for new bites. I decided to count my bites, since my skin was peppered with them, but I lost count after about one hundred thirty three. A bit of petroleum jelly on many of them seemed to take away the itch—perhaps because the ointment sealed off the bites from the air. Mercifully, none were infected yet, even though infections on the skin happen incredibly fast in this tropical coastal climate.

Buzzing human conversations soon gave way to buzzing jungle sounds, and the little thatched house seemed to be surrounded by a never-ending cascade of night critter sounds. We heard high-droned mosquitoes very close to our ears, perhaps frustrated because they could not reach our tender skin through the net. We tuned in to spasmodic messages from various kinds of crickets, interspersed with spooky sounds from hooting owls. Village dogs yapped and howled for a while, but gradually their noises subsided.

At last the village slept.

twenty

BURSTING THE BANKS

Lae boasts an annual rainfall of two hundred or more inches. This statistic made for interesting conversations when we were home on leave, especially when speaking in a state like Texas, where the annual rainfall was the same as we could get in one night in Lae. There are some distinct advantages, however. First, it's usually unnecessary to go out and water one's flowers. Moreover, spectacular orchids grow and nod from tree trunks in incredibly beautiful, delicate sprays. Besides, it was always a new surprise to watch our "dead" fence posts sprout into huge trees in the course of a couple of years.

The downside of this statistic is that roads can turn into soggy quagmires, which strain the axles of even the best-built cars. Moreover, black mildew sprouts and spreads on white ceilings, while white mildew grows on dark colored wood doors. One chemical cleaner whose manufacturers insisted that it killed such unsightly growth, seemed to act as a catalyst, and not a deterrent, for the spread of mildew on our ceilings.

One rainy season we planned a staff retreat and decided to hold the daytime sessions in the spacious living room of Lae International High School. This school sits amid beautiful shady trees near the banks of the Bumbu River. The school had a dormitory for boarders and a well-equipped kitchen. Sixty-five participants arrived for the retreat, and we all headed for the school in cars and vans, taking along all the food we would need to prepare and cook there for the two days of retreat.

Saturday morning brought heavy rain, but we hardly noticed, as we were concentrating on the Bible studies and discussions of the morning. At noon we ate lunch together there, and then continued our sessions. The rain persisted relentlessly, coming down in torrents. We looked out the large windows, and noticed enormous puddles everywhere. But we couldn't see the river from there, so we didn't realize how it was creeping up.

Meanwhile, some of us went into the kitchen to peel potatoes and to prepare meat and vegetables for the evening meal. Just as the last potatoes lost their skins, the phone rang—it was a miracle in itself to have the phone still working after all that rain. Don, a friend from across the river, where we lived, and where all the participants were to sleep that night, spoke anxiously.

"We've already had about 15 inches of rain," he said, "and it shows no signs of letting up. The river is rising awfully fast."

"We are fine here and are keeping dry indoors," we assured him.

"But the bridges might not hold," he replied. "The approaches may not be safe. You'd better come back to this side right away."

"Can't we wait until we've cooked all this food and eaten it?"

"Well, I don't think that's a safe idea. Some of the people here say they've never seen the river so high before."

"OK. We'll pack up and come as soon as possible. Thanks for the warning. 'Bye."

We told the group we would all leave and continue our retreat on the other side. *Where can we meet? We haven't booked a place on that side of the river. What place will hold sixty-five retreat participants?*

"What about all this food?" someone asked.

"Let's take what we need for tonight, and leave all of tomorrow's food here, because we'll come back and have tomorrow's sessions here anyway, won't we?"

"Sure, but how will we carry all these peeled potatoes?"

"Just throw them into the big pots, and take along the meat and vegetables, and we'll cook everything over at the guest house and at our place," I said.

So we piled people and peeled potatoes into the vehicles, jumped in, and drove off into the darkness, and into the deafening rain. We inched our way toward the bridge, saw that it was still intact, and drove across. We gasped at the roiling, deathly torrent on either side of the van, and watched through the rear windows as the other vehicles made their way across.

As we drove along, we saw people streaming along the road, weighed down with loads of bags and pots and other items. The river banks had burst, and many homes were under water. They were all streaming towards Ampo, our destination, in hopes of finding higher ground and safety. What a bedraggled, struggling, wet ribbon of humanity wound its way along the road! Our cars were packed full, so we could not stop for anyone; besides, there were hundreds of them. But we knew we had to help them find food and shelter as soon as possible.

Arriving at Ampo, we dropped people off at our house and at the guest house, where the manageress graciously allowed us to cook some of the food.

A few minutes later Don came by to see if we were there. He looked pale.

"The bridge approaches just washed away. There's a 30-foot gap between the road and the bridge."

We stared at one another in disbelief, in fear, in relief, and in awe. *Thank you, God! We are safe! All sixty-five of us are safe!* Then we wondered about others. Was there any vehicle on the bridge when it went? Waves of relief washed over all of us when we heard no one had been on the bridge at that moment.

By now it was dark, and the food was almost ready. We gathered together plates from our house and from the guest house kitchen, and were ready to serve the somewhat delayed evening meal.

A knock at the door revealed a neighbor to say that the second bridge's approaches had just washed away too, and that people were continuing to stream into Ampo from their settlement, which by now was under water. While some in the community looked for shelter for the refugees, others of us raided our refrigerators and cupboards for food, and none of us felt much like eating our meal. We ate a little, and we put a lot of the food into the big pots, adding whatever we could find in our own houses to cook up huge pots of thick, nutritious soup. Someone came and loaded these pots into a car, and then took them down to the buildings where the people were sheltered.

The rain kept up its relentless downpour, and by midnight we'd had 21 inches. We almost forgot about retreat sessions, but somehow everyone was pretty good-natured about the state of affairs. Saturday night was to be a light night anyway as far as sessions were concerned. The out-of-town participants bedded down in our homes, and soon everything grew quiet.

I could now begin worrying in earnest. *What will we give everyone for breakfast? How can we fetch all that food for Sunday from the other side of the swollen river? How can we buy food when the stores are on the other side and the bridges are gone? What are the retreat participants going to say when there is nothing to eat? Why did we cook and give away all that food for the soup tonight?* Ron assured me not to worry, and that things would work out, but I was the hostess now, and I wasn't going to let anyone stop me from worrying. Finally, however, we slept.

Sunday dawned. Birds chorused the arrival of a new day, and no rainfall accompanied their songs. What a miracle—this birth of a fresh new day after a torrent of rain. Water lay everywhere, but the heaviest rains had stopped.

The kitchen cabinet held enough flour and other ingredients for me to make muffins for breakfast, and I found plenty of coffee, so everyone had something to eat. We worshiped together and continued our retreat. Later in the day we all went to the river to survey the damage.

The flood waters had retreated somewhat by afternoon, but there was no way for us to get to the other side. We prayed that no one would need a doctor or a hospital, or would need to fly anywhere. Our own retreat participants found enough to do to keep themselves occupied while waiting for a way to leave Lae and return to their homes. Engineers busied themselves with plans to bulldoze the riverbanks enough for a walking path to be formed, as soon as floodwaters had receded sufficiently.

Our problems, however, paled in comparison with those of the settlement folks, whose homes and goods had been swept away by the flood waters. For weeks these people stayed in inadequate shelters. Despite our donations toward helping our displaced neighbors, I felt guilty about having such a nice big house when so many people had no place to live. Should we open our house to let some families shelter here? If so, which ones? How would the others feel about that? How long would they stay? If they moved in, what would we do about other people who often stayed with us when they were visiting town for medical care, shopping trips, and meetings? The flood and its aftermath led to much unease and soul-searching.

Thanks to a generous gift of tents from the Australian government, a new settlement called "Tent City" sprang up about eight miles out of town, and more than eight hundred displaced persons began a new chapter of their lives.

We were amazed as we watched these people make the best of their circumstances. Within a short time they were building little shanties and digging the ground, getting ready to plant some food. Soon little mounds of sweet potato plants surrounded the tents, interspersed with delicate corn plants, spring onions, and leafy greens. Our river neighbors had lost their dwellings, their animals, and most of their personal goods; yet here they were, hand-tilling the soil, working the ground, and looking ahead. With further assistance from churches, the government, and the army, "Tent City" developed roads, a fresh food market, and, eventually, an elementary school. Tents gave way to more permanent buildings, and the new community established leadership and organization.

twenty-one

MUNCHING ON THE ROCK

"Guess what!" exclaimed my fellow instructor, "The student teaching supervision list is out. Do you know where you'll be going?"

"No. Let me run and look."

I hurried to the faculty room and checked the wall. I found my name next to the name of Gantom Community School. Hmm! "Where is that?" I asked.

"Oh, it's just a few miles out of town, not too far from the University of Technology."

Just then the deputy principal of the college came in. "Else, I hope that you won't mind driving the truck every day with the students for Gantom. You've had a lot of experience driving the trucks, and we are short of drivers."

"Do I just keep the truck with me all day while supervising the students?" was my next question.

"Sure, unless we need the truck for something else during the day. On such days our maintenance man will take you out there first and then pick you up later in the afternoon."

"That sounds fine to me."

A few days later, I met with my group of fifteen young men and women who were to carry out their student teaching at Gantom. Some were first year students ready for their very first experience of "block teaching," as we called it. Others were second year students, almost ready to graduate, and somewhat knowledgeable in the area of student teaching. During our meeting together the students filled out some basic information such as where they were from, what grades, if any, they had taught during previous times of student teaching, and what responsibilities they would have within the group. We would spend four rather intensive weeks together. They were each assigned to a classroom under the immediate supervision of the regular teacher of that room, and over the four-week period they would slowly assume more and more of the lessons. I tried to visit every student for at least nine lessons during that time, watching the lessons, writing evaluations, and giving feedback each time. My schedule for each day was thus packed as I tried to utilize every minute to help the students during this valuable time of student teaching. Lessons were short, especially in the lower grades, so I was bobbing in and out of classrooms all day long. Some classrooms had a rickety chair for me at the back or side of the room, while others had a spare half desk for me to squeeze into, and in other rooms I perched on a stool. By the third week I tried to watch a block of several lessons of each student, and that was not quite as hectic for me.

Driving out to Gantom became a daily adventure. Traffic was often heavy, since we left at seven in the morning, just when hundreds of people were walking, riding, driving, or bicycling to school and to work. As we headed out of the city, jungle-covered mountains in the distance provided a spectacular backdrop for our journey. Large banana trees, coconut palms, and flowering casuarina trees flanked our road, and a colorful assortment of vehicles, some chugging along with us, others coming from the opposite direction, provided endless sources of conversation for those of us privileged to be in the front cab of the truck.

Meanwhile, in the back of the open truck, the other students, clutching their lesson plans and hanging tightly onto their posters and other home-made teaching aids on their windblown ride, laughed and sang their way along to Gantom.

The first couple days of student teaching were always a little awkward, since we didn't know the teachers, much less the pupils, and we were never sure whether we would get along with them or not. But the classroom teachers and their student teachers quickly bonded, and usually the students had very positive experiences during those weeks.

Gantom Community School had the privilege of a super captain in the person of its principal, Ms. Suitawa. What superb learning we gained from her caring, competent, professional leadership. She exhibited the marvelous knack of running a very organized school while showing compassion and friendship to every teacher and every student. Whenever a teacher was ill at the last minute and couldn't come to school, she'd promptly step in and take the class until an arrangement could be made with another teacher to double up for a few hours. Their school system did not allow for the luxury of calling for a substitute teacher.

Gantom nestled on the slope of foothills on the outskirts of a suburban area called Taraka. Classrooms encircled a central square, which served as a sloping, outdoor gymnasium for the sports enthusiasts. Physical education classes formed an essential part of the curriculum, as did music and religious education. All instruction took place in English, the official language of the country, but in the lower grades, teachers sometimes used the local language to help children over some early hurdles with learning English.

The structure and quality of classrooms at Gantom varied considerably. Several classroom blocks were built from sturdy permanent materials, with low fibrolite walls about a yard or meter high, open air above that level, and iron roofs. Other classrooms were of thatched bush materials, including woven bamboo walls, thatched grass roofs, and smooth, somewhat lumpy dirt floors. I frequently seemed to end up supervising in the back of one of these classrooms whenever the rains came, and we often moved around during such lessons, trying to dodge the splatters from leaks in the thatched roof. The children remained amazingly cheerful and good-natured throughout such rainy interludes.

Furniture in the classrooms included little desks for upper grades and nothing for first graders. The latter sat cross-legged in rows on little pieces of pasteboard on the floor, balancing their slates and books. They'd rise in a flash when their teacher recommended an action song, a mime, a role play to illustrate some grammatical construction, or a science experiment out under the trees. Each teacher had a desk somewhere in the classroom; parents had built some of the desks, while others came from a furniture store.

Precious few books lined these sparse classrooms, and children often shared textbooks. In some classes at least three children shared one reader. Children made mobiles, art posters, and coconut leaf origami projects which adorned every section of the classroom. One corner proudly exhibited a rock collection, an insect collection, and a few sturdy round "bush" balls constructed from tightly wound lengths of vines. Every morning classroom monitors swept the classrooms with brooms made from shredded coconut leaves. These pliable spines of coconut leaves, when bundled together in a bunch of about one hundred, with one end tied by a sturdy length of vine, made super, albeit short, brooms.

Gantom School's grounds boasted spectacular flowering shrubs as well as multi-colored leafy shrubs around every classroom. Daily, between the first and second bells, children weeded and cleaned around the flower beds. The bell was a relic, a contraption which used to be an oxygen cylinder during the Second World War. Upper class children enjoyed having a turn at ringing the school bell by banging on it with a large bolt or other metal object.

Each day as lunchtime approached, clusters of mothers plus a few fathers began to arrive from all over the area, trudging up the hill, a *bilum* or string bag full of food hanging from their heads and resting on their stooped backs. As each mother arrived under a shady tree, she carefully spread out a grass-woven mat or a sheet of plastic on the smooth earth, swung her bag off her back, carefully sat down cross-legged in front of the mat, and began unloading her goodies.

Some mothers brought a large hot pot full of boiled rice; others brought green cucumbers; yet others had a pot full of corn cobs which had been roasted in ashes. Those who had fruit trees in their yards carried *bilums* full of succulent dainties such as fresh guavas, thick golden bananas, tiny red India rose apples, or huge juicy slices of pineapple. As they lined up these foods on their mats, the mothers would chatter and laugh together, sharing stories and swapping baby experiences.

At twelve noon someone banged the gong, and within seconds jovial wiry youngsters came catapulting out of classrooms, clutching a few *toea* (pennies), and heading straight for the lunch "tables." Laughing and pointing, they chose an item from the mat, handed over their coins, and dashed off with their friends to sit in a shady place and consume their lunch. Soon another bell sounded, and kids jumped up and ran off to play ball for the rest of lunch hour. Then, just before coming back for afternoon classes, they all lined up by the only water faucet on campus to douse their perspiring faces with water and take in a deep drink.

Our students bonded almost instantly with these children, who treated the strangers with tremendous enthusiasm and awe. My students spent many lunch hours teaching the children the rules for new games, and showing them unique ways to fashion a new toy or game from forest materials. Children in their turn taught us new ways to recycle precious school supplies and to make teaching materials from the surrounding forest.

My lunch seat during these weeks was an uncomfortably pointy rock situated under a scrawny tree near the school's entrance. Unfortunately, a colony of red ants shared this spot with me on some days, so I usually stomped my feet around in a semi-circle while eating. I could have eaten inside a classroom, but the action took place outdoors during lunch break, and the people's activities provided endless fascination and learning for me. Besides, I was within view of my students without hovering over them, and many times during lunch hour some of them wandered over to me with a question or a concern, needing a bit of reassurance, or checking my schedule for the time I would next observe them. Also, the regular teachers saw me as a professional guest who was always available for questions or discussions, but who didn't hover and "inspect" everything, nor demand a fancy chair in some office.

Special times included tea break with the staff—a luxury which the teachers permitted themselves only a couple of times a week, because tea and cookies cost money, and money was scarce. During these teatimes we enjoyed a special camaraderie with these dedicated, extremely busy teachers. A couple of times I baked a huge batch of sweet rolls at home and brought them along to share at teatime. They were a great hit.

In mid-afternoon, at the end of the school day, as the children cheerfully made their way toward their homes, my students and I piled into the truck and began our drive back to our college in Lae. Many times, our groups of student teachers were assigned much farther away. In such cases, they and their supervising instructors stayed with host families near the school and returned only at the end of their four-week student teaching period. We continually gained new insights from these powerful learning experiences.

twenty-two

THE FINAL *MUMU*

In the Southern Hemisphere, the end of the school year often falls early in December, at the onset of the summer months. In Papua New Guinea, even though we were only a few degrees south of the equator, we felt ourselves firmly entrenched in the Southern Hemisphere, and thus we followed the school year dates of such countries as Australia and New Zealand.

At Balob Teachers College in Lae, early December annually marked graduation, a significant and moving rite of passage for our teacher education students and for the whole college community. Our students hailed from as many as nineteen different provinces of the country. They spoke an aggregate of thirty to forty different languages, and came from cultures as varied and diverse as persons from entirely differing continents. During their years of study at Balob, these young people from all over the country studied, worshiped, and ate together daily, shared dormitory rooms, and agonized together over incredibly difficult problems as their family and their country underwent immense changes.

Time drew near for the graduating students to separate, to find teaching positions in the far-flung communities in the country, and to face even harsher realities than those they'd faced as young adults at college.

Papua New Guineans traditionally form family and clan communities and make decisions through intensive discussion leading to consensus. Coming to Balob provided them with the Western, not-always-the-best alternative of committee meetings, in which resolutions passed by majority vote and not necessarily by consensus. We often found ourselves accommodating both kinds of decision-making. First, we would hear interminable discussion of a resolution by every committee member until we were pretty sure that everyone was in agreement; then we would put it to a vote and hope that there were no dissenting votes. And often, there weren't, except occasionally from an expatriate faculty member such as someone from the United States or Australia.

Graduation activities needed planning many months ahead of the actual date. Committees formed early in the last semester of school, and these included a program committee, a decorations committee, a dinner committee, a refreshments committee, a speaker-selection committee, and a baccalaureate service committee, among others.

Often, most students were away from campus for about a month of continuous student teaching just before graduation, so much of the planning had to be in place before they left campus. They traveled in groups of twelve and fourteen, together with one or two faculty supervisors, to community schools in the province. There, staying with host families in the villages, they had their student teaching experience under the guidance of regular teachers stationed there in the villages.

Once this "block" teaching time was over, the rush was on, and frenzied activity took the place of usual regular routines at the college. Food committees gathered to choose the menu, the method of cooking food for five hundred persons, the places and means for buying the ingredients, and volunteers for cutting food, cooking, serving, and cleaning up.

Students from the Central Highlands of Papua New Guinea gathered to discuss plans for making a Highlands-style *mumu.* First, they negotiated with a nearby plantation to purchase and butcher a cow. Next, the day before the graduation dinner, they dug a deep, wide pit on the college grounds. One load of students went with the truck to a nearby river and picked up a load of round white stones. They brought these back to the site and carefully lined the hole with these stones. Another group negotiated with landowners near the forest to buy and gather firewood for cooking.

Before dawn on the morning of the graduation dinner, nimble young men clambered up coconut trees on the college grounds or in the yards of faculty members (this was all pre-arranged), and shook down dozens of green coconuts. Others, wielding machetes, slashed down long green branches from banana trees which dotted the college grounds. Another group climbed coconut trees again to cut long green coconut fronds for decorating the basketball court for their festive dinner. Some of the women walked, barefooted, to hedges and flowering trees, carefully cutting and picking a wealth and variety of exotic hibiscus blooms, orchids, fragrant frangipani blossoms, and long elegantly curved bougainvillea branches, laden with delicate purple and maroon-colored blossoms, to add to the decorations.

At the same time that early morning, students piled firewood across wooden bars which spanned the cooking hole, and set alight the wood. As the fire burned the logs, it also burned the wooden bars holding up the rest of the firewood, and soon these pieces fell into the ground. Quickly, the students added more firewood and covered the hole with banana leaves, letting the fire heat up the white stones.

Meanwhile, students had cut big slabs of beef, while others peeled hundreds of sweet potatoes, yams, and taro. Another group sliced onions and washed and cut big wedges of green cabbage. A few had gathered a pile of coconuts and were cutting them open with a big bush knife, catching the clear sweet coconut water in a pail. Some of the women sat astride narrow benches, which had a jagged metal grater at one end, and they grated the snow-white flesh of the coconut on this stool. Soon a hill of shredded coconut filled the big dish beneath the grater, and the women carefully wrapped piles of this coconut into clean white cloths, twisted the cloths, and extracted thick, creamy white coconut milk this way.

With dexterous rhythm and speed, these young people carefully transported the huge dishes of food near the hole. While some opened the hole and cleaned it out, using long wooden sticks—for the stones were red hot by now—others carefully lined the stone-lined hole with long green "tablecloths" of banana leaves. Then gently, men laid slabs of beef all over the hole, interspersed with yams, sweet potatoes, and taro. Over each lot of food, they then laid large chunks of cabbage mixed with sliced onion. Then someone carefully poured thick coconut milk over the pile.

All this while the stones sizzled as wet food and coconut milk touched them. Excitedly, the young men and women covered all the food with extra banana leaves, and then gingerly piled some more hot stones over the top, using long thin wooden sticks as tongs. Finally, they spread another layer of wide, green banana leaves over the top of the heap. Then, as someone held a stick right in the center of the hole, others began piling sand and dirt over everything. At the command of the man in charge of this operation, the stick in the center was lifted out, and someone poured a pail of water down the hole. The water sizzled and splattered as it hit the hot stones. Quickly, they covered this hole, too, allowing the food to steam between hot stones, mingling scrumptious flavors in the process. Carefully they placed the stick back in, covering the area around it with sand, in order to seal in the heat.

For now, the *mumu* had to work by itself, and students moved away to take a break from the hot work and to talk about how good it would taste in a few hours.

Back in the college kitchen, students were busy washing and cutting fresh cucumbers, papaya, pineapples, and other vegetables. Some were cutting up chickens and greens to drop into big pots for stewing.

Meantime, members of the decorating committee, recruiting some additional volunteers among students and family members of faculty and staff, began transforming the grey slab of concrete which formed our basketball court. Whittling bark off some saplings, they pounded them into the ground at regular intervals all around the court. Within minutes, they tied together long shredded fronds of coconut leaves and fastened these to the saplings. This formed a ring of coconut fronds all around the basketball court. But the job was not finished. Soon, children, laughing and singing, tied flowers and blossoms to the sheet of coconut fronds, and these gently waved in the breeze, sending little breaths of exotic fragrance over the whole court.

Another crew of students soon appeared, dragging long thin logs and mats woven from coconut leaves. They dropped these at various spots around the outside of the court, and proceeded to build table-like platforms, with attached benches, as seats for people.

Everywhere an air of expectancy and excitement prevailed. Soon, tantalizing tendrils of flavor exuded from the *mumu* pit.

After a few hours, the *mumu* was ready, and as guests began to gather, walking in from all over the town, the cooking crew removed sand and banana leaves, carefully lifted out the food, piece by piece, using long thin sticks, and showed amazing dexterity as they avoided breaking the tender pieces of food. They carried this food in large wide dishes to the newly-constructed serving tables and gently piled the food onto fresh green banana leaf tablecloths lining the platforms. They covered all the food with additional banana leaves. Meanwhile, the pots of food from the mess also arrived.

As students gathered, staff and faculty and families, together with special guests and speakers, mingled among them, visiting, sharing news, sniffing the air redolent with food cooked *mumu*-style.

We sat down around the court, cross-legged, clutching a plate, a fork, and a drinking mug. The college principal welcomed everyone, and the chaplain had an opening prayer. Then, while we lined up near our designated platform—each faculty adviser and family sat with his or her advisees and any of these students' relatives—a talented group from the Madang area entertained everyone by singing and playing guitars. Later, when the assembled people felt pleasantly satisfied and relaxed, more entertainment began. There were speeches and awards, and between these items, various groups of students and children performed traditional dances, sang traditional songs, and put on short or long dramas and amusing mimes. We felt like the sixteenth century English who were privileged to attend Shakespearean plays in the open-air theaters.

A graduation meal at Balob became a symphony of community cooperation. The instruments included tolerance and acceptance, food, and willingness to sacrifice a lot of time. The players were young women and men at the threshold of a new life, with a variety of talents and interests and commitment, which they brought together in planning this dinner for an appreciative audience—their family members, their instructors, their fellow-students, and their neighbors.

EPILOGUE

Ron and I, together with our children, left Papua New Guinea in 1991 after serving there together for twenty-six life-transforming years. Arriving back in the United States, we searched for a table around which to build our new community, and, to our delight, we found a sturdy wooden dining room table with well-fashioned chairs to match. Countless times we have added chairs to the circle, and whenever we have run out of chairs, pillows and floor space have worked very well.

In 1992, we moved to Dubuque, Iowa, returning to the city where Ron and I had begun our married life thirty years earlier. Though grieving for our Papua New Guinea community, we looked forward to becoming part of a new neighborhood. Through our work and studies at Wartburg Theological Seminary, we have found a special, caring community, one which embodies its faith and teachings through worship, active community events, projects involving justice issues, and involvements beyond its walls to the city, the country, and the world. Wartburg's students from the United States and from many other countries of the globe continue to enrich our lives and expand our insights in many ways.

Other nurturing communities include those at Holy Trinity Lutheran Church as well as the participants of the Tuesday Noon Ecumenical Bible Study at St. Mark's Community Center. These friends provide precious insights as well as prayer support through thick and thin.

Whenever we gather around a table or in a circle with others, be it at home or at a church potluck, at the house of friends or at a meeting, in a park or in a restaurant, we celebrate community in a fresh way. We continue to learn new, grace-filled lessons about life and faith, and for these we give thanks daily.

Our honeymoon home at Wartburg Seminary in Dubuque, Iowa,
1962-1965

The *M.V. Simbang* entering the harbor at Finschhafen

Butaweng Swimming Pool, Finschhafen

Our Family in Lae, Papua New Guinea, 1984
Back: Heidi, Natalie, Graham
Front: Joy, Else, Ron

Balob Teachers' College students cooking a crocodile *Mumu*-style in our back yard in Lae.

Else Schardt with student teachers from Balob Teachers' College

A new community with international students and friends at our home in Dubuque, Iowa